Patricia East
Brian McCredie

Besser in Englisch

9. Klasse

Cornelsen
Power Learning

Diese Lernhilfe gibt es auch mit CD-ROM:
Cornelsen Power Learning Englisch 9. Klasse
(ISBN 3-589-21512-7)

Cornelsen online http://www.cornelsen.de

Gedruckt auf chlorfrei gebleichtem Papier
ohne Dioxinbelastung der Gewässer.

Bibliografische Information
Die Deutsche Bibliothek verzeichnet diese Publikation in der Deutschen Nationalbibliografie; detaillierte bibliografische Daten sind im Internet über **http://dnb.ddb.de** abrufbar.

Dieses Werk berücksichtigt die Regeln der reformierten Rechtschreibung und Zeichensetzung.

6.	5.	4.	3.	2.	Die letzten Ziffern bezeichnen
08	07	06	05	04	Zahl und Jahr der Auflage.

Redaktion: Helga Holtkamp, Sigrid Janssen, Jill Kitchen, Susanne Schütz
Gesamtgestaltung: Dagmar & Torsten Lemme, Berlin
Umschlagentwurf: Bauer + Möhring, Berlin
Illustrationen: Roland Beier, Berlin; Kathrin Schwertner, Berlin
Repro: City Repro, Berlin
Druck und Bindung: Tesinska Tiskarna, Cesky Tesin
Printed in the Czech Republic
ISBN 3-589-21820-7
Bestellnummer 218207

Inhalt

Vorwort

Liebe Schülerin, lieber Schüler!
Du hast hier ein Buch zum Lernen, Wiederholen und Üben in der Hand.
Die Themen sind in kleinen, verständlichen Schritten aufbereitet.
An vielen Stellen kannst du selbst in das Buch hineinschreiben.
Kontrolliere deine Ergebnisse mit dem Lösungsheft.

Mit diesem Buch kannst du auf *zweierlei Weise* arbeiten:

1. **Möglichkeit:**
   Du fühlst dich insgesamt in Englisch unsicher. Dann arbeite das Buch von vorne bis hinten durch. Nimm dir nicht zu viel auf einmal vor. Bearbeite lieber kleinere Abschnitte, aber dafür regelmäßig, vielleicht sogar täglich.

2. **Möglichkeit:**
   Du kennst deine Lücken. Du weißt, bei welchen Aufgabenstellungen du noch unsicher bist. Dann sieh im Inhaltsverzeichnis nach, picke einzelne Abschnitte heraus, und arbeite sie durch.

Und noch einige praktische Tipps zum Lernen mit diesem Buch:

- Verwende zum Eintragen ins Buch einen Bleistift. Fehler kannst du dann leichter ausbessern.
- Bist du dir beim Lösen der Übungsaufgaben nicht ganz sicher, sieh dir die Beispiele noch einmal genau an.
- Vergleiche deine Ergebnisse mit dem Lösungsheft. Überprüfe bei Fehlern immer genau, was du falsch gemacht hast.
- Bearbeite die Übungsaufgaben nach einigen Tagen noch einmal. So kannst du zusätzliche Sicherheit gewinnen.

Die *Symbole* am Seitenrand bedeuten:

Wichtige Regel:
Präge sie dir genau ein.

Überprüfe, ob du
den Stoff schon beherrschst.

Übungsaufgabe:
Löse sie im Buch oder Heft.

Beispiel:
Es zeigt dir, wie es richtig ist.

1 *Present* und *past*

A Das *simple present* und das *present progressive*

B Das *simple past* und das *past progressive*

C Das *simple past*, das *present perfect* und *present perfect progressive*

D Das *past perfect* und das *past perfect progressive*

A Das *simple present* und das *present progressive*

❶ Everybody **pays** taxes to the Government.
❷ Marilyn **works** as a nurse.
❸ This film **deals** with race relations.
❹ His plane **leaves** Heathrow airport at 8 a.m.
❺ Where's Ralph this evening? He's **working** on a new project.
❻ Next Saturday he's **attending** a conference on developing countries.

▷ Simple present:	I, you, we, they	live
	he, she, it	live**s**
▷ Present progressive:	I	**am** liv**ing**
	you, we, they	**are** liv**ing**
	he, she, it	**is** liv**ing**

▶ Das *simple present* wird für gewohnheitsmäßige Handlungen und bei Berufen verwendet ❶ ❷.

Das *simple present* wird außerdem für die Darstellung von Tatsachen verwendet ❸.

Das *simple present* wird für künftiges Geschehen verwendet, wenn dieses durch einen Fahrplan, Stundenplan o. Ä. festgelegt wird ❹.

▶ Das *present progressive* drückt aus, was jemand gerade im Moment macht ❺.

Das *present progressive* in Verbindung mit einer entsprechenden Zeitangabe drückt eine zukünftige Handlung aus ❻.

Exercise 1

Ashrafs Familie stammt aus Indien, aber die Kinder sind alle in England aufgewachsen. Die Familie führt ein Lebensmittelgeschäft im Londoner Stadtteil Streatham. Ashraf gibt ein Interview für die Fernsehsendung „London Today" und erzählt aus dem Alltag seiner Familie.

Setze die richtigen Verbformen ein.

~~check~~ – ~~do~~ – work (2 x) – decorate – do – help out *(aushelfen)* – drive – deliver – send – train – stand – specialize *(spezialisieren)* – stay – choose – live – clean – come

1 Hello! Pleased to meet you all! Come into the shop. I 'm checking a few bills at the moment. My father usually does this, but it's my job today.

2 The tax inspector *(Steuerbeamte)* ____________ next Monday, so everything must be in order!

3 My brother Hamid and I are in charge today. He ____________ vegetables to Mrs Belson at the moment. She's nearly ninety, you know. She sometimes ____________ her fruit and vegetables herself, but when the weather's bad like today she ____________ at home and ____________ one of her grandchildren, and Hamid ____________ round in the van.

4 That's my cousin, the pretty one that ____________ at the till *(Kasse)*. She ____________ with us at the moment. She ____________ to be a nurse at Guy's Hospital.

5 Two of my sisters ____________ as nurses, and one of my cousins is a doctor. He ____________ in heart diseases and at the moment he ____________ some research *(Forschung)* on heart problems in small children.

6 That guy who ____________ the shop window? Oh, he's a friend of ours – he ____________ here regularly. He always ____________ when we're really busy.

7 It's a pity you couldn't come next week. We ____________ the whole shop on Sunday, and everything will look a lot better then!

B Das *simple past* und das *past progressive*

❶ A terrible accident **happened** at this crossroads last week.
❷ When they **heard** the explosion, the firemen **threw** themselves to the ground and **covered** their heads.
❸ What **was** she **doing** at 10 o'clock last night? She certainly **wasn't waiting** for me at the airport.
❹ When the riot **started**, I was **sitting** at home.

▷ Simple past: I live**d**

▷ Past progressive: I **was** liv**ing**

▶ Das *simple past* wird verwendet, um zu berichten, dass etwas zu einer bestimmten Zeit in der Vergangenheit passiert ist ❶.

Das *simple past* wird auch für eine Reihe von Handlungen verwendet, die nacheinander passierten ❷.

▶ Das *past progressive* wird verwendet, um zu erzählen, was zu einer bestimmten Zeit in der Vergangenheit passiert ist ❸ oder was gerade im Gange war, als etwas geschah ❹.

Exercise 2

In der Vergangenheit kam es immer wieder zu Rassenunruhen in Städten wie Liverpool.

Setze die richtige Verbform ein.

~~receive~~ – hurry – not waste – arrive – ~~stand~~ – shout – not take – happen – try – go on *(vor sich gehen)* – reach – see – kick – punch *(schlagen)* – look up – notice – take – turn – disappear – follow – leave – not move – breathe – moan *(stöhnen)*

1 As soon as the police received the emergency call, they ______________ to Toxteth, the area of the riot. They ______________ a minute.

2 When they ______________, a crowd was standing in the middle of the street and somebody ______________ 'Nigger! Nigger!'

3 It ______________ long for the police to find out exactly what ______________, even though so many people ______________ to see what ______________.

4 When the policemen finally ______________ the middle of the crowd, they

__________ a small group of youths who __________ and __________ a well-dressed black man.

5 Suddenly one of the youths __________ and __________ a cameraman who __________ photographs of him. He __________ round and __________ into the crowd before anybody could stop him. The others __________ him and __________ the black man, who __________ any longer. But he __________ still __________ and __________ quietly when they found him.

Exercise 3

1972 kamen etwa 30.000 Asiaten aus Uganda nach Großbritannien.
Sie waren aus Uganda vertrieben worden.
Einer von ihnen beschreibt seine Ankunft am Londoner Flughafen Heathrow.

Setze die richtigen Verbformen ein. Manchmal musst du das Passiv verwenden.

1 When we came through customs, we saw hundreds of people who were waiting (wait) for friends and relatives.

2 I looked into the crowd and __________ (try) to spot *(entdecken)* my sister.

3 At last I saw her. She __________ (wear) a red sari *(indisches Frauengewand)* and __________ *(stand)* next to the exit.

4 When she saw me she __________ (wave) and __________ (call) my name.

5 All around us people __________ (laugh) and __________ (cry) with relief at seeing their relatives safe again.

6 "We were very worried about you when we __________ (see) the news on TV", she said.

7 "It was impossible to escape sooner", I said. "Yesterday I __________ (drive) to the airport and __________ (wait) for nine hours, but all the flights to England __________ (cancel = *streichen*). There were so many people there, and a lot of them __________ (not get) a ticket at all. I was one of the lucky few."

C Das *simple past*, das *present perfect* und *present perfect progressive*

❶ The English **conquered** *(erobern)* Ireland in the twelfth century.
❷ When **did** the Irish Republic **become** independent?
❸ The newspapers **have reported** every detail of the scandal, so everybody knows all about it now.
❹ The Prime Minister **has** already **held** one press conference this week, and he may decide to hold another.
❺ I **haven't heard** any news since Tom arrived/for 24 hours.
❻ – **Has** the Government **found** a solution to the problem yet?
– No, it **has decided** to carry on the discussion next week.
❼ – How long **has** the Government **been dealing** with this problem now?
– The Government **has been discussing** this problem for years.
❽ What have you **been doing** to my kitchen? It looks like a battlefield *(Schlachtfeld)*.
– Sorry about the mess but **I've been cooking** an exotic meal.

▷ Present perfect:	I **have** lived he **has** lived
▷ Present perfect progressive:	I **have been** living he **has been** living

- ▶ Das *simple past* wird für abgeschlossene Handlungen verwendet, die zu einem bestimmten Zeitpunkt oder in einem bestimmten Zeitraum in der Vergangenheit passierten ❶, oder wenn man nach einem Geschehen fragt, das eindeutig in der Vergangenheit liegt ❷.

- ▶ Das *present perfect* wird verwendet, wenn etwas passiert ist oder jemand etwas getan hat, ohne dass erwähnt wird, wann sich dieser Vorgang ereignet hat. Der **Zeitpunkt**, zu dem sich der Vorgang ereignet hat, ist also **unwichtig**. Wichtig ist nur, dass in der Gegenwart ein **Ergebnis** des Vorgangs vorliegt ❸.

  Dieser Bezug zwischen Vergangenheit und Gegenwart wird häufig durch Zeitadverbien wie *already, ever, never, since* (seit + Zeitpunkt), *for* (seit + Zeitraum) und *yet* verdeutlicht ❹ ❺ ❻.

- ▶ Das *present perfect progressive* wird für Vorgänge verwendet, die in der **Vergangenheit begonnen** haben und bis in die **Gegenwart** (möglicherweise auch in der Zukunft) **andauern** ❼.

  Das *present perfect progressive* wird auch verwendet, wenn eine Handlung in der **Vergangenheit**, die nicht weit zurückliegt, zu unbeabsichtigten **Folgen** in der **Gegenwart** geführt hat ❽.

▶ Während mit dem *present perfect* eher Fragen nach **Ergebnissen** gestellt und beantwortet werden ❻, werden mit dem *present perfect progressive* Fragen nach den **Tätigkeiten** selbst gestellt und beantwortet ❼.

Exercise 4

Lies den Text sehr sorgfältig durch und kennzeichne dann die darauf folgenden Sätze.

✔ = richtig ✘ = falsch

Manche sind grammatikalisch falsch und manche entsprechen nicht den Fakten, die im Text stehen. Kannst du auch erklären, was nicht stimmt?

Ireland tried hard to win some form of independence throughout the nineteenth century. In 1922 the country was divided: Southern Ireland, with a Catholic majority, became the Republic of Ireland (Eire), and Northern Ireland, with a Protestant majority, remained a part of the United Kingdom. Although there was peace in Northern Ireland for nearly 50 years, the Protestants discriminated against the Catholics in many ways. The Catholics protested with the Civil Rights Movement in the sixties. Protestant extremists were afraid of a reunion *(Wiedervereinigung)* with Eire and began to attack Catholics in Belfast and other towns.
In 1969 the British Government sent troops to support the police there.
In spite of several attempts *(Versuch)* to reach a political solution, no answer to the conflict has yet been found, and violence and terror on both sides have continued ever since. Thousands of people have already lost their lives.

1 Ireland has tried hard to win some form of independence throughout the nineteenth century.

2 Ireland has been divided since 1922.

3 Southern Ireland has become the Republic of Ireland in 1922.

4 The UK has administered *(verwalten)* Northern Ireland as part of the UK for over 80 years.

5 There <u>has been</u> peace in Northern Ireland for 50 years.

6 The Civil Rights Movement <u>has protested</u> against discrimination in the sixties.

7 The British Government <u>has stationed</u> troops in Northern Ireland since 1969.

8 Nobody <u>has solved</u> the conflict yet.

9 The violence <u>caused</u> thousands of deaths.

Exercise 5

Setze die richtigen Verbformen ein. Manchmal musst du das Passiv verwenden.

1 In 1976 two women, Betty Williams and Mairead Corrigan, established (establish) a Peace Movement.

2 The two women ____________________ (receive) the Nobel Peace Prize a year later.

3 The Peace Movement only ____________________ (exist) for a few years. It ____________________ (die) when people ____________________ (realize) that a simple wish for peace ____________________ (not be able) to end the violence.

4 The situation in Northern Ireland ______________________________ (get) worse since the British ____________________ (send) troops in in 1969.

5 The IRA (Irish Republican Army) wants to reunite Ireland. It ______________________________ (not accept) any solution suggested by the Government so far.

6 The British see the IRA as terrorists, but the IRA members ______________________________ (always insist) that they are freedom fighters.

7 How many people ______________________________ (kill) since the Troubles ____________________ (begin)?

8 ____________________ (you see) the documentary film that ____________________ (show) on TV last night?

9 Some people who are now politicians ______________________________ (support) the IRA.

10 For many years people in Ireland and in the UK ______________________________ (hope) for a solution to the problem.

Exercise 6

Since oder *for*? Streiche jeweils das falsche Wort durch.

1 Racial discrimination has been illegal in Britain since/for 1968.

2 Lots of foreign workers have had a job in Germany since/for a long time.

3 Apartheid existed in South Africa since/for over forty years.

4 Have the newspapers published any photos of Lawrence since/for his operation?

5 Nothing has been heard of the terrorist since/for he was arrested.

6 At the age of nineteen, Gandhi went to England to study law *(Jura)* at London University since/for several unhappy years.

D Das *past perfect* und das *past perfect progressive*

❶ Most of Britain's colonies had become independent before 1970.
❷ After they had travelled all day Ryan fell over his suitcase and broke his ankle.
❸ How long had you been waiting before you received your work permit?

▷ Past perfect: I had lived

▷ Past perfect progressive: I had been living

▶ Das *past perfect* wird verwendet, um Ereignisse zu beschreiben, die zu einem bestimmten Zeitpunkt in der Vergangenheit **abgeschlossen** waren ❶.

Wenn zwei aufeinander folgende Ereignisse in der Vergangenheit beschrieben werden, wird das *past perfect* verwendet, um das **weiter zurückliegende Ereignis** zu beschreiben. Die darauf folgende Handlung steht im *simple past* ❷.

▶ Das *past perfect progressive* wird verwendet, um Vorgänge zu beschreiben, die bis zu einem bestimmten Zeitpunkt in der Vergangenheit noch **andauerten** ❸.

Exercise 7

Setze die richtigen Verbformen für das *simple past*, das *past perfect* und das *past perfect progressive* ein.

1 Last month Mr Miller ________________ (lose) his job.

2 He ______________________________ (work) for the company for seven years.

3 They ________________ (buy) their house only the month before and Mrs Miller ____________________________________ (decorate) the living room when her husband ___________ (tell) her the bad news.

4 They ________________ (work) very hard to buy the house and Mrs Miller ________________ (give up) her job as a teacher to work on the renovation.

5 There ______________ (be) some money that Mr Miller's father ______________ (leave) them after his death but they ____________________ ___________________ (plan) to save it.

6 Until Mr Miller ______________ (become) unemployed they ______________ (spend) the summer holidays on a Greek island and ________________________ ______________ (also be able) to go skiing in winter.

Test

Exercise 1

Der erste Satzteil lässt sich jeweils mit einem der angegebenen Satzteile zu einem sinnvollen Satz verbinden.
Unterstreiche den passenden Satzteil.

✔ = richtig ✘ = falsch

1 I switched on the TV
when the news began.
when the news has begun. ✔

2 When he pulled the emergency brake *(Notbremse)*
the train stops.
the train stopped.
the train has stopped.

3 Martin doesn't know about the accident because
he hadn't read the news yet.
he hasn't read the news yet.

4 India has been independent
for over 50 years.
since over 50 years.

5 Until he became a nurse at Guy's Hospital
Ashley worked in a small clinic.
Ashley has worked in a small clinic.

6 The Sullivans moved back to Dublin
after Mr Sullivan has stopped working for the police.
after Mr Sullivan had stopped working for the police.
after Mr Sullivan was working for the police.

7 When I arrived at the station
lots of people were waiting for relatives to arrive.
lots of people waited for relatives to arrive.

8 Call an ambulance!
The boss had a heart attack *(Herzinfarkt)*!
The boss has had a heard attack!
The boss was having a heart attack!

9 Scarlet didn't hear what the teacher said
because she was listening to her walkman.
because she listens to her walkman.
because she has listened to her walkman.

max. 8

Exercise 2

Setze die richtigen Verbformen ein. Manchmal musst du das Passiv verwenden.

Lawrence is a travel reporter. He ________________ [1] (write) for a magazine called 'People and Places'. He ________________ [2] (spend) most of his time doing research for his articles. At the moment he ________________ [3] (travel) through the Himalayas and he ________________ [4] (collect) ideas and material for his next book.

At present he ________________ [5] (plan) a report on a town in Eastern Nepal which ________________ [6] (shake) by an earthquake a year ago. Hundreds of people ________________ [7] (kill) immediately, and thousands more ________________ [8] (die) of hunger since then. Many people ________________ still ________________ [9] (live) in temporary huts. They ____________________________ [10] (not rebuild) their houses yet because they still ____________________________ [11] (not receive) the money that the Government ________________ [12] (promise) them when the earthquake ________________ [13] (destroy) their villages. Lawrence ________________ [14] (be worried) about the children. They ________________________ [15] (not eat) proper food for a long time. Two years before the earthquake the villagers ________________ ________________ [16] (finish) building a new school. All the children ________________ ________________ [17] (go) to this school but now they ________________________ __________ [18] (not even have) a proper home.

max 18

Weniger als 21 Punkte? Wenn ja,
arbeite bitte Kapitel 1 nochmals durch!

gesamt max. 26

2 Das Futur

A Das *will-future* und das *going to-future*

B Das *simple present* und das *present progressive*

C Das *future progressive*

A Das *will-future* und das *going to-future*

❶ Space flights **will continue** until man is master of the universe.
❷ Don't stop learning English now. You'**ll regret** *(bedauern)* it later.
❸ – I've forgotten my umbrella.
– Don't worry. I'll lend you mine.
❹ – **Maybe** the Government **will introduce** a new law on CO_2 emissions after the next election, but I'**m** not **sure** they **will**.
❺ I'**m going to write** a letter to 'The Times' tomorrow and complain about the traffic jams on the motorways.
❻ Look at those black clouds! It's **going to rain**.

▷ Will-future:	will + infinitive	
▷ Going to-future:	I am he is you are	+ going to + infinitive

▶ Das *will-future* wird verwendet für **Aussagen** über zukünftige Geschehen, auf die man keinen Einfluss hat ❶, um **Vermutungen** über die Zukunft zu äußern ❷ oder wenn man sich im Augenblick des Sprechens **spontan** zu etwas **entschließt** ❸.

▶ Oft verwendet man mit dem *will-future* Adverbien wie *maybe, perhaps, probably* sowie Verben und Ausdrücke wie *believe, imagine, suppose, think, be sure,* um Vermutungen über die Zukunft zu äußern ❹.

- Das *going to-future* wird verwendet, wenn wir über **Pläne und Absichten** sprechen, die wir selbst bestimmen können ❺. Es wird oft in Verbindung mit Zeitbestimmungen wie *now, tomorrow, this year, next week* verwendet.
- Das *going to-future* wird auch verwendet, um auszudrücken, dass etwas mit **Sicherheit oder großer Wahrscheinlichkeit** bald passieren wird. Meistens gibt es schon Anzeichen dafür ❻.

Exercise 1

Marc und seine Freundin Anna sind überzeugt, dass sie etwas für ihre Umwelt tun sollten. Sie diskutieren darüber mit ihren Klassenkameraden.
Hier ein Ausschnitt aus ihrem Gespräch.

Will oder *going to*? Setze die richtige Zeitform ein.

1 *Marc* It's time to stop talking and start doing something about our environment. We' re going to start (start) a 'Save the Forests' project at school.

2 *Anna* I think I' ll make (make) a list of things we could do. ________ you ________ (lend) me your pen, Marc?

3 *Sarah* Millions of tons of plastic are produced every day. Think how much plastic there ________ (be) in the world if we carry on using so much of it! I've decided that from now on *(ab jetzt)* I ________ (not use) anything except cotton bags for my shopping.

4 *Peter* I don't think our personal efforts *(Bemühung)* ________ (make) much difference.

5 *Lyndon* Well, I suppose the world ________ (not be changed) immediately by our ideas, but somebody's got to start. If we don't make a start, who ________? I think some people ________ (be influenced) by what we do.

6 *Marc* Anna and I ________ (put up) a poster in our local supermarket. I'm sure that at least people ________ (think) about what they're buying if we remind them about the environment.

7 *Tracey* Perhaps my mother ________ (have) some useful suggestions – she's a member of the 'Friends of the Earth' organization, you know.

8 *John* Let's go and ask her straight away. Do you want a lift home, Tracey? I ________ (take) you on my bike.

Exercise 2

Will-future oder *going to-future*?
Übersetze die fehlenden Satzteile.

1 The world's oil reserves will last (*werden ausreichen*) about another 30 years.

2 A lot of people __________ probably ____________________ (*werden … nie ändern*) their habits.

3 The Government ____________________ (*wird … einführen*) tax reductions for those using power (*Strom*) produced by alternative energy sources next year.

4 I ____________________ (*werde aufhören*) using plastic bags from now on!

5 People _______________ (*werden … verbrauchen* = use) less energy because it has become too expensive.

6 Solar energy has the advantage that the sun ____________________ (*immer scheinen wird*).

7 The Prime Minister ____________________ (*wird sprechen*) about energy conservation on TV tomorrow.

8 I wonder what people in the next century _______________ (*denken werden*) about nuclear energy.

9 A lot of nuclear power plants _____________________________ (*werden geschlossen werden*) in the next few years.

10 Look at those lorries! They ____________________ (*werden beginnen*) building the new underground soon.

B Das *simple present* und das *present progressive*

❶ The plane from London **arrives** at 9.00 the day after tomorrow.
❷ Next weekend I'**m taking part** in a TV discussion on sources of energy.
❸ I'll ring you when I **arrive**.

- Genau wie im Deutschen wird das *simple present* gebraucht, um über **planmäßige Vorgänge** (Fahrpläne, Arbeitsstunden, Stundenpläne usw.) zu sprechen ❶.
- Bei feststehenden künftigen Ereignissen wird in Verbindung mit einer **Zeitangabe der Zukunft** statt des *going to-future* auch das *present progressive* verwendet ❷.
- In einem **Gliedsatz**, der durch *as soon as, before, if, until, when* eingeleitet wird, benutzt man **immer** das *simple present* und **niemals** *will* oder *going to* ❸.

Exercise 3

Vervollständige die folgenden Sätze mit der richtigen Zeitform des angegebenen Verbs.

1 A government official is coming (come) to our school next Thursday to talk about environmental problems.

2 The film show about acid *(sauer)* rain doesn't start (not start) until 7.30.

3 I'm sure you'll be interested in my idea for saving seals *(Robben)* when you ____________ (find out) more about it.

4 We ____________ (take part) in a demonstration against the pollution of the North Sea next month.

5 The environmentalist Bob Cole will come if he ____________ (be able to).

6 I can't make any plans until I ____________ (know) what you want.

7 What ____________ (you do) this weekend?
I'd love to see you if you ____________ (have) time.

8 At Christmas my American boyfriend ____________ (come) to stay, and next summer holiday I ____________ (fly) to the USA to visit him.

9 My plane ____________ (leave) very early in the morning.

10 There will be more protests if they ____________ (not stop) building that recycling plant.

C Das *future progressive*

❶ This time next week I'**ll be working** for my exams.
❷ **Will you be watching** the late-night film at 11.00?

▶ Das *future progressive* wird verwendet, um auszudrücken, dass etwas zu einer bestimmten Zeit in der Zukunft vor sich gehen wird.

Exercise 4

Nach einer Bergwanderung in den schottischen Highlands ruhen sich zwei Wanderer in einer Berghütte aus. Ein Einheimischer erzählt ihnen, wie sich alles im nächsten Jahr verändern wird, denn das Gebiet soll für den Tourismus erschlossen werden.

Bilde Sätze mit dem *future progressive* aus den vorgegebenen Satzteilen.

1 Where you're standing now/team of workmen/build/big hotel

Where you're standing now a team of workmen will be building a big hotel.

2 they/transport/lots of lazy people/to the top of Ben Nevis/by cable-car *(Seilbahn)*

____

____

3 thousands of people/breathe/fresh mountain air/and enjoy/the countryside

____

____

4 and thousands of others/drop/litter/all over the mountains

____

____

5 And what/I/do/in the middle of all this?

____

____

6 I expect/I/tell/people like you how beautiful these mountains used to be a year ago!

____

____

____

Test

Übersetze die fehlenden Satzteile mit einer passenden Verbform mit futurischer Bedeutung.

✔ = richtig ✘ = falsch

1 Wenn das Eis am Nordpol schmilzt, wird die Temperatur überall steigen.

If the ice at the North Pole ______________________________,

the temperature ______________________________ everywhere.

2 – Was machst du am Wochenende? – Ich fahre nach Berlin.

– ______________________________ at the weekend?

– ______________________________ to Berlin.

3 Ab dem 1. Januar werde ich nicht mehr rauchen.

From January 1st I ______________________________.

4 Roger zieht nach London, sobald er mit der Schule fertig ist.

Roger ______________________________

______________________________.

5 In England fängt die Schule um 9 Uhr an. Wann fängt sie in Deutschland an?

In England school ______________________________.

When ______________________________ in Germany?

6 Die Alpen werden vom Tourismus zerstört werden, wenn wir nicht bald handeln.

The Alps ______________________________

unless we ______________________________.

7 Kommst du morgen zu der Demonstration gegen die Verschmutzung der Flüsse?

______________________________ demonstration

against river pollution tomorrow?

8 Nächstes Jahr um diese Zeit sitze ich bestimmt nicht hier mit meinen Grammatikbüchern!

This time next year I certainly ______________________________

with my grammar books!

9 Lass uns etwas für unsere Umwelt tun, bevor es zu spät ist!

Let's do something for our environment ______________________________

______________________________!

10 Die meisten Autofahrer werden nicht langsamer fahren, bis die Regierung eine Geschwindigkeitsbegrenzung *(speed limit)* einführt.

Most drivers ______________________________

until the Government ______________________________.

11 Falls ich meine Prüfungen nicht bestehe, werde ich wahrscheinlich noch ein Jahr an der Schule bleiben.

If I ______________________________ my exams,

I ______________________________ at school for another year.

12 – Ich finde mein Englischwörterbuch nicht.

– Keine Sorge, ich leihe dir meins.

– I can't find my English dictionary.

– Don't worry, I ______________________________ you mine.

Weniger als 15 Punkte? Wenn ja, arbeite bitte Kapitel 2 nochmals durch! max. 19

3 Die indirekte Rede

A Verschiebung der Zeiten

B Veränderung der Pronomen und Adverbien

C Fragen

D Aufforderungen, Bitten und Ratschläge

E Vorschläge

A Verschiebung der Zeiten

❶	*Sarah* “It’s difficult to find a suitable job in Liverpool.” Sarah **said** (that) it **was** difficult to find a suitable job in Liverpool.	simple present ▼ simple past
❷	*John* “I’m trying to get a part-time job.” John **told me** (that) he **was trying** to get a part-time job.	present progressive ▼ past progressive
❸	*Hugh* “I’ve spent hours writing job applications.” Hugh **complained** (that) he **had spent** hours writing job applications.	present perfect ▼ past perfect
❹	*Michelle* “I worked in my father’s shop for two weeks.” Michelle **mentioned** (that) she **had worked** in her father’s shop for two weeks.	simple past ▼ past perfect
❺	*Steve* “I was helping Joe to find a job on the Internet.” Steve **explained** (that) he **had been helping** Joe to find a job on the Internet.	past progressive ▼ past perfect progressive
❻	*Stanley* “I’ll stay on at school if I pass my exams.” Stanley **commented** that he **would stay** on at school if he passed his exams.	will ▼ would
❼	*Kate* “I’m going to be a bank clerk.” Kate **said** (that) she **was going** to be a bank clerk.”	going to-future ▼ was/were going to + infinitive
❽	*Sue* “I can type but I can’t do shorthand.” Sue **emphasized** (that) she **could** type but (that) she **couldn’t** do shorthand.	can ▼ could

- Wenn in der indirekten Rede das einleitende Verb im *simple past* steht *(he said, he told us, …)*, verschiebt sich die Zeitform der direkten Rede um eine „Zeitstufe“ zurück ❶ – ❼.
- Die modalen Hilfsverben *could* (= könnte), *might, should, would* bleiben unverändert ❽.

- Die wichtigsten Verben, die die indirekte Rede einleiten, sind: *answer, claim, comment, complain, emphasize, know, mention, report, say, stress, tell, think, write.*

Exercise 1

Setze die richtigen Verbformen ein.

1 *Sam* “I want to leave school as soon as possible.”

Sam said (that) he _wanted_ to leave school as soon as possible.

2 *Ashley* “I’m learning to type at evening classes.”

Ashley told us (that) he ________________ to type at evening classes.

3 *Alexa* “I’ve applied for jobs with local firms, but I’ve always been turned down.”

Alexa commented that she ________________ for jobs with local firms, but

____ .

4 *Paul* “I’ve decided to try to get into university.”

Paul mentioned (that) he ________________ to try to get into university.

5 *Sally* “The careers officer *(Berufsberater)* discussed my ideas with me, but he didn’t have any good suggestions.”

Sally complained (that) the careers officer ________________________ her ideas with her, but he ________________ any good suggestions.

6 *Ted* “I’ll make sure I’m punctual for my interview.”

Ted emphasized (that) he ________________ sure he ________________ punctual for his interview.

Exercise 2

Rashid ist 18 Jahre alt und wohnt in Birmingham. Seine Eltern kommen aus Indien. Seit einem Jahr ist er ohne Arbeit.
Es ist gerade ein Artikel über arbeitslose Jugendliche wie Rashid in einer deutschen Zeitung erschienen.
Hier sind Auszüge aus dem Artikel.

Übersetze die fehlenden Satzteile. Verwende folgende einleitende Verben:

complain – emphasize – add – say – think

1 Rashid beschwerte sich, dass manchmal Minderheiten auf dem Arbeitsmarkt in Großbritannien diskriminiert würden.

Rashid complained that minorities were sometimes discriminated against on the job market in Great Britain.

2 Er betonte, dass Minderheiten schon immer in vielen Gesellschaften schlecht behandelt worden seien.

He ______ that minorities in many societies ______ always ______ badly.

3 Er fügte hinzu, dass er bei vielen Firmen Arbeit gesucht habe und dass seine Erfahrungen nicht immer angenehm gewesen seien.

He ______ that he ______ work at lots of firms and his experiences ______ always ______ pleasant.

4 Rashid sagte, er würde einige Agenturen anrufen, die er im Internet gefunden habe.

Rashid ______ that he ______ a few agencies he ______ on the Internet.

5 Er meinte, er könnte durch die Agenturen eine Stelle bekommen, wenn er Glück hätte.

He ______ that he ______ a job through the agencies if he ______ lucky.

B Veränderung der Pronomen und Adverbien

❶	*Secretary*	"We moved into our new office three days ago, so everything is really untidy."
	Pat (a week later)	"The secretary said (that) **they** had moved into **their** new office **three days before**, so everything was really untidy."
❷	*Steven*	"I'll call you tomorrow about the interview."
	Sandra (five days later)	"Steven promised (that) **he** would call me **the next day** about the interview, but he never rang."
❸	*Marion*	"We can meet here again next week."
	Paul (a month later)	"Marion suggested (that) we could meet **there** again **the following week**."

▶ Wie im Deutschen muss man immer bedenken, dass aus der Sicht des Berichtenden Ort, Zeit und Personen anders erscheinen als in der direkten Rede.

▷ **Demonstrative pronouns**

this	that
these	those

Adverbs of place

here	there

Adverbs of time

now	then
today	that day
yesterday	the day before/the previous day
two days ago	two days before
last week	the week before/the previous week
tomorrow	the next/the following day
next week	a week later/the following week

Exercise 3

Die folgenden Sätze ergeben keinen Sinn, weil die unterstrichenen Pronomen und Adverbien falsch sind.
Setze die richtigen Formen ein.

1 Jim went to Bristol to look for a job as a computer salesman.
Yesterday he phoned and said I *he* had found a fantastic job here *there*.

2 Last Sunday Sally told me I ________ had received bad news about her A-level marks yesterday ________________________.

3 *Interviewer* "Yes, Mr Green, you've got the right qualifications to work for our company."
Mr Green "The man who interviewed me said you ______________ had the right qualifications to work for my ________ company."

4 The boss promised that she would let me have tomorrow ____________________ ________ off, and then she wondered why I wasn't at work!

5 I spoke to Mr Lotus and Mr Bentley at the meeting last Friday and them ________ told me we ___________ had sacked three of the staff two days ago.

C Fragen

❶ *Mrs B* "Why did you give up your training course, Susan?"
Mrs B asked Susan **why she had given up** her training course.

❷ *Mrs B* "Are you interested in a career *(Karriere)* as an actress, Pauline?
Mrs B asked Pauline **whether/if she was interested** in a career as an actress.

- ▶ Wenn das einleitende Verb im *simple past* steht, gilt die Regel über die Verschiebung der Zeiten auch für Fragesätze.
- ▶ Die Wortstellung bleibt bei Fragesätzen in der indirekten Rede die gleiche wie bei Aussagesätzen.
- ▶ Beginnt die direkte Rede mit einem Fragewort *(why, when, how, usw.)*, wird das Fragewort in die indirekte Rede übernommen ❶.
- ▶ Wenn die direkte Rede kein Fragewort enthält, steht *if* oder *whether* in der indirekten Rede ❷.

▷			Subjekt	Verb	Objekt
	She asked	whether if	I	had given up	my job.

▷ Einleitende Verben in Fragesätzen sind z. B. *ask, want to know, wonder*.

Exercise 4

Jill möchte als Au-pair-Mädchen arbeiten und stellt sich bei einer Agentur vor. Später berichtet Jill über das Gespräch mit Mrs Knight von der Agentur. Vervollständige ihren Bericht.

1 Mrs Knight asked me *whether this was* the first job *I had applied for*. I told her it was.

2 She asked ______________________ as an au pair before, and I answered that I ______________ plenty of experience with my little brother.

3 She asked ______________________ French, and I told her I ______________ four years of French at school.

4 She wanted to know ______________________ work, and I said I ______________ whenever she ______________ .

5 Then I asked her how much free time ______________________ , and she said I ______________________ every afternoon off and the whole day on Fridays.

D Aufforderungen, Bitten und Ratschläge

❶ *Mr Smith* "Switch on the video recorder, Sam."
Mr Smith **told Sam to switch on the video recorder**.

❷ *Mr Smith* "Don't send them another e-mail, Tim."
Mr Smith **told Tim not to send them another e-mail**.

❸ *Paul*" Will you help me with the questionnaire, Anita?"
Paul **asked Anita to help him with the questionnaire**.

❹ *Ms Blackley* "Take my advice, Sheila: become an air hostess."
Ms Blackley **advised Sheila to become an air hostess**.

▶ Aufforderungen ❶ ❷, Bitten ❸ und Ratschläge ❹ werden in der indirekten Rede mit dem Infinitiv gebildet. Die verneinte Form wird mit *not to* + Infinitiv gebildet ❷.

Exercise 5

Setze die folgenden Aufforderungen, Bitten und Ratschläge in die indirekte Rede.
Benutze jeweils das Verb in Klammern als einleitendes Verb.

1 *Boss* "Sue, book a hotel in York for me, please." (ask)

The boss asked Sue to book a hotel in York for him.

2 *Director* "Thomas, give me a report after the meeting." (instruct)

The director ______________________ him a report after the meeting.

3 *Alan* "Janice, please photocopy the new brochure immediately". (ask)

Alan ______________________ the new brochure immediately.

4 *Manager* "Don't forget to bring the documents, Liz!" (tell)

The manager ______________________ to bring the documents.

5 *Teacher* "I think you should do computer studies *(Informatik)* at A-level, James." (advise)

The teacher ______________________ computer studies at A-level.

6 *Tom* "You're welcome to use my computer any time, Katy." (invite)

Tom ______________________ his computer any time.

E Vorschläge

Mrs Topham "Shall we employ a new assistant in the boutique?"
Janet "Good idea! Let's ring the job centre straight away."

❶ Mrs Topham **suggested employing** a new assistant in the boutique, and Janet **suggested ringing** the job centre straight away.
❷ Mrs Topham **suggested that they employed** a new assistant in the boutique, and Janet **suggested that they rang** the job centre straight away.
❸ Mrs Topham **suggested (that) they should employ** a new assistant in the boutique, and Janet **suggested (that) they should ring** the job centre straight away.

▶ Auf *suggest* folgt entweder eine *-ing*-Konstruktion (Gerundium) ❶, *that + simple past* ❷ oder *(that) + should/could + infinitive* ❸.

Exercise 6

Ken, Tricias Vater, macht einige Vorschläge für die Zukunft seiner Tochter. Tricia erzählt nachher ihrer Freundin, was er gesagt hat.

Vervollständige ihre Erzählung mit einer der drei Strukturen, die auf *suggest* folgen.

Ken Well, you've got plenty of alternatives. You can stay on at school if you like; or you could leave school now and go on a training course; or you could go abroad for a year to practise your languages; or you could stay at home and help me in the family business.

Tricia **1** Dad suggested *staying on/that I stayed on/should/could stay on* at school.

2 He also suggested ______ school now and ______ on a training course.

3 Then he suggested ______ abroad for a year to practise my languages.

4 And he even suggested ______ at home and ______ in the family business. But I'd hate that!

Test

Exercise 1

Vor der Parlamentswahl äußern sich die Kandidaten zu ihren Plänen für die Bekämpfung der Jugendarbeitslosigkeit.

Vervollständige die folgenden Sätze.

✔ = richtig ✘ = falsch

1 The Liberal Democrat candidate

said that his party would improve youth training schemes ✔

2 The Conservative candidate said

____

3 The Green Party candidate promised

____

4 The Labour Party candidate promised

____

5 The Silly Party candidate advised everybody

____

max 11

Exercise 2

Vervollständige folgende Übersetzungen.

1 Mrs Bones sagte, ihre Firma beschäftige über 100 Sekretäre und keiner habe sich jemals über seine Arbeitsbedingungen beklagt.

Mrs Bones said her company ______________________________ over 100 secretaries

and none of them __________________________ ever ____________________________

about their working conditions.

2 Der Firmenleiter schlug vor, eine Zweigstelle in München zu gründen *(set up)*.

The manager _______________________ ____

a branch in Munich.

3 Die Verkäuferin fragte, wann ich den Computer gekauft hätte.

The sales assistant ______________________________ when

______________________________ the computer.

4 Tom erzählte mir, er habe gelernt, den neuen Drucker zu bedienen, und habe vor *(intend)*, in Zukunft alle seine Berichte selber zu drucken.

Tom ______________________________ me he ______________________________ to

use the new printer and ___________________________________ to print out all

his reports himself in future.

5 Die Assistentin riet mir, mich rechtzeitig für den Kurs anzumelden *(register)*.

The assistant ______________________________ me

____ for the course in good time.

max. 11

Exercise 3

Übertrage folgende Sätze in die indirekte Rede.

1 *Jenny* "If I were you, I would hire a new assistant."

She advised me ______________________________ a new assistant.

2 *Nurse* "The surgeon has operated on ten patients today."

(A week later) The nurse said that the surgeon ____________________________

on ten patients __________________________ .

3 *Tom* "I am going to apply for a place at London University. Why don't you apply, too?"

Tom told me that _________________________________ for a place at London

University and he suggested that I __________________________ , too.

4 *Pat* "Bob, would you lend me your video over the weekend?"

Pat asked Bob _________________________________ video over the weekend.

5 *Reporter* "Several architects are designing a new conference hall. Next month the committee *(Ausschuss)* will decide who to give the contract to."

The reporter informed us that several architects __________________________

a new conference hall, and that the committee ___________________________

__________________________ who to give the contract to.

6 *Rick* "Sam worked for a TV company for five years, but he quarrelled with his boss. Now he's working as a postman."

Rick explained that Sam ________________ for a TV company for five years, but

_________________________________ with his boss. He added that now he

__________________________ as a postman.

max 12

Weniger als 22 Punkte? Wenn ja, arbeite bitte Kapitel 3 nochmals durch!

gesamt max 27

4 *If*-Sätze

A *If*-Sätze im *simple present* (Typ 1)

B *If*-Sätze im *simple past* (Typ 2)

C *If*-Sätze im *past perfect* (Typ 3)

A *If*-Sätze im *simple present* (Typ 1)

❶ If Mr Muscles **wins** the marathon, he'**ll get** a gold medal.
❷ You **can earn** a lot of money through advertising if you **succeed** as a sportsman.
❸ If you **see** Moira tonight, **ask** her to phone me.
❹ You'll never improve **unless** you train harder.
❺ If any more trouble **is caused** by our football fans, our team **will be banned** from international matches.

▷ *if*-Satz	Hauptsatz
if + *simple present*	*will-future* ❶, Hilfsverb + Infinitiv ❷ oder Imperativ ❸

- In *if*-Sätzen, in denen das Verb im *simple present* steht, nennt der Sprecher eine Bedingung, die aus seiner Sicht erfüllbar ist. Im Hauptsatz steht dann die Folge, also was passiert oder passieren wird, wenn die Bedingung erfüllt ist.

- Der *if*-Satz kann vor oder nach dem Hauptsatz stehen. Steht er vor dem Hauptsatz, wird er vom Hauptsatz durch ein Komma abgetrennt ❶.
- *Unless* kann anstelle von *if ... not* stehen ❹.
- In *if*-Sätzen wird das Passiv nach den gleichen Regeln wie bei anderen Satzformen gebildet (eine Form von *be* + Partizip Perfekt = 3. Form) ❺.

Exercise 1

Ein Tennistrainer ist mit seiner Mannschaft nicht zufrieden und er versucht, sie zu besseren Leistungen anzuspornen.

Setze die Verben ein.

~~not do~~ – ~~lose~~ – take – start – go – do – improve – hit – hold – get – concentrate – not select *(Passiv)*

1 You've lost the first five matches of the season! If you _don't do_ anything about it, you _'ll lose_ the rest, too!

2 If you ____________ my training programme seriously, you ____________ looking like real tennis players.

3 If you ____________ running and ____________ one hour of exercises every day, you ____________ your performance enormously.

4 You ____________ the ball much harder if you ____________ your racket properly, and you ____________ all the difficult shots *(Schläge)* if you really ____________ on the ball.

5 Anyone who shouts at the umpire *(Schiedsrichter)* ____________ for the team.

Exercise 2

Alles richtig gemacht in Übung 1? Dann vervollständige diese Sätze, indem du *unless* und das richtige Verb einsetzt.

1 The trainer says the team won't start looking like real tennis players _unless they take_ his training programme seriously.

2 He says they won't improve their performance ____________ running every day.

3 He says you can't hit the ball hard ____________ your racket properly.

4 And you can't get all the difficult shots ____________ really ____________ on the ball.

B *If*-Sätze im *simple past* (Typ 2)

❶ If I **won** the lottery, I **would travel** round the world.
❷ If I **had** more money, I **could buy** myself a computer.
❸ If I **was** older, I **might** be rich.
❹ If the rules **were always obeyed**, fewer athletes **would be disqualified**.

▷ *if*-Sätze	Hauptsatz
if + simple past	*would/could/might + infinitive*

▶ In *if*-Sätzen, in denen das Verb im *simple past* steht, nennt der Sprecher eine Bedingung, deren Erfüllung aus seiner Sicht unwahrscheinlich ist ❶ oder deren Erfüllung unmöglich ist ❷ ❸. Im Hauptsatz steht dann die Folge, also was passieren würde oder könnte, wenn die Bedingung erfüllt würde/werden könnte.
Das *simple past* im *if*-Satz hat nichts mit der Vergangenheit zu tun.

▶ Merke dir die Passivformen ❹.

Exercise 3

Fritz Meier, Vorsitzender eines Sportvereins, gibt ein Interview für eine englische Zeitschrift zum Thema „Sport und Geld". Seine Antworten werden ins Englische übersetzt.

Übersetze die unterstrichenen Satzteile.

1 *Interviewer* Every sport is being taken over by professionals. What do you think about this development?

Fritz Meier Es ist unvermeidbar: Wenn Sportler weniger verdienen würden, könnten sie nicht so viel leisten.

If sportsmen ___earned___ less, they ___couldn't___ achieve so much.

2 *Interviewer* Why?

Fritz Meier Ganz einfach. Ein Sportler könnte nicht an der Spitze bleiben, wenn er nicht jeden Tag trainieren würde.

A sportsman ______________________________ stay at the top ______________________________ every day.

3 *Interviewer* Couldn't he train after work?

Fritz Meier Er hätte weder Zeit noch die Energie, wenn er auch noch arbeiten müsste.

He ____________________ neither the time nor the energy if he ____________________ work as well.

4 *Interviewer* Would sportsmen do their best if they did not expect such high financial reward?

Fritz Meier Ein Sportler würde gewinnen wollen, auch wenn er kein Preisgeld erhalten würde.

A sportsman ____________________ even if he ____________________ any prize money.

5 *Interviewer* Would sport still be sponsored by advertising if there were fewer professionals?

Fritz Meier Amateure würden gesponsert werden, wenn sie genug Zuschauer anziehen *(attract)* würden.

Amateurs ____________________ if they ____________________ enough spectators.

C *If*-Sätze im *past perfect* (Typ 3)

❶ If I **had won** the match, I **would have been** the champion.
❷ I **could have seen** Mr Muscles if I **had been** on that plane.
❸ If I **had asked**, somebody **might have helped** me.
❹ He **would have been injured** if he **had been kicked** harder.

▷ *if*-Satz	Hauptsatz
if + past perfect	*would/could/might have + past participle* (3. Form)

▶ In *if*-Sätzen, in denen das Verb im *past perfect* steht, nennt der Sprecher eine Bedingung, deren Erfüllung nicht mehr möglich ist, weil das Beschriebene schon passiert ist. Im Hauptsatz steht dann, was passiert wäre, wenn …

▶ Merke dir die Passivformen ❹.

Exercise 4

Ausschreitungen sind bei Fußballspielen eine häufige Begleiterscheinung. Russel Smythe, Sportschaumoderator, überlegt sich nach einem von Ausschreitungen überschatteten Spiel, was man hätte tun können.

Setze die Verben ein. Pass auf: Manchmal musst du das Passiv verwenden!

> ~~take~~ – ~~imagine~~ – control – not be – have – be – search – have –
> forbid – be – avoid – separate – be – be able

1 The stadium has been damaged and cars and shop windows have been smashed. I'm sure the organizers *would have taken* more effective measures if they *had imagined* what some people are capable of doing.

2 If the club ______________ the sale of tickets, some of the hooligans ______________ in the stadium at all.

3 If we ______________ stricter security regulations, there ______________ less trouble.

4 If everyone ______________ when they entered the stadium, nobody ______________ knives or bottles with them.

5 If the sale of alcohol ______________, fewer people ______________ drunk.

6 Some of the violence inside the stadium ______________ ______________ if the supporters of the two teams ______________ ______________.

7 And lastly, if there ______________ more policemen, they ______________ to keep control.

Exercise 5

Nach dem Tennisendspiel in Wimbledon gibt die Siegerin im Dameneinzel (Renate Stamm) ein Interview für das britische Fernsehen. Vervollständige ihre Antworten, indem du die unterstrichenen Satzteile übersetzt.

1 *Reporter* Congratulations! Tell us, how did you become such a great player? Is it all just natural talent?

Renate Also, Talent und ein guter Anfang, glaube ich. Wenn mein Vater mir das Tennisspielen nicht beigebracht *(teach)* hätte, sobald ich laufen konnte, hätte sich mein Talent nicht so schnell entwickelt *(develop)*.

If my father ______________________________ me to play tennis as soon as I could walk, my talent ______________________________ so quickly.

2 *Reporter* Was it your father who helped you most?

Renate Eigentlich meine ganze Familie. Ich wäre nie so gut geworden, wenn sie mir nicht so viel Unterstützung gegeben hätte.

I ______________________________ so good if they ______________________________ me so much support.

3 *Reporter* How about today's game: did you feel confident all the time?

Renate In jedem Spiel gibt es ein bisschen Glück. Wenn ich Pech gehabt hätte *(to be unlucky)*, wäre alles schief gegangen *(go wrong)*.

If I ______________________________ , everything ______________________________ .

4 *Reporter* You were the favourite at Wimbledon this year. Did the crowd's support help you?

Renate Ich glaube, ich hätte gewonnen, auch wenn die Zuschauer nicht auf meiner Seite gewesen wären. Aber es ist immer ein schönes Gefühl, wenn sie einen mögen!

I think I ______________________________ even if the spectators ______________________________ on my side.

Exercise 6

Es hätte anders sein können!
Bilde jeweils einen *if*-Satz aus den vorgegebenen Sätzen. Beginn mit dem *if*-Satz.

1 I couldn't go to the match because I didn't have a ticket.

If I had had a ticket, I could have gone to the match.

2 I didn't buy new jogging shoes because I didn't have enough money.

3 I was unlucky. That's why I lost the match.

4 Sally trained too hard when she was a child. That's why she damaged her spine *(Wirbelsäule)*.

5 There was a terrible accident because the racing car turned over.

6 The match was cancelled because it rained all day.

7 The football star moved to Monaco because he had to pay such high taxes in his own country.

Test

Typ 1	*if + simple present*	*will-future*, Hilfsverb + Infinitiv, Imperativ
Typ 2	*if + simple past*	*would/could/might* + Infinitiv
Typ 3	*if + past perfect*	*would/could/might have + past participle*

Exercise 1

Setze die richtigen Formen der in Klammern vorgegebenen Verben ein.

✔ = richtig ✘ = falsch

1 If there ________________ (be) less youth unemployment, football hooliganism would not be such a problem.

2 If you ________________ (join) a tennis club, you can play whenever you like.

3 If you ________________ (switch on) the TV news last night, you ________________________________ (be able to) see the highlights *(Höhepunkt)* of the match.

4 If manufacturers ________________ (reduce) the price of sports equipment, I ________________________ (buy) new things more often.

5 Would the number of spectators at the football stadiums ________________ (go down) if football matches ________________ (be broadcast) live on TV?

6 Would you ________________________ (take part) in the city marathon last year if you ________________ (recover) from your injury?

7 Unless sport and politics ________________ (be) kept seperate, the Olympic Games ________________ (became) a political battlefield.

8 I ____________________ (have to) train harder if I had wanted to become a professional.

9 As a tennis player you ________________ (not earn) much for advertising unless you ________________ (be) very successful.

10 If I ________________ (know) you would be there, I ________________ ________________ (attend) the meeting.

max. 17

Exercise 2

Vervollständige die folgenden Sätze, indem du die Satzteile in Klammern übersetzt.

1 I can't take you with me, *(wenn du nicht bis 8 Uhr fertig bist.)*

____

2 There might be less football hooliganism, *(wenn man im Stadion keinen Alkohol kaufen könnte.)*

____

____

3 Wimbledon would be less exciting, *(wenn professionelle Spieler nicht teilnehmen würden.)*

____

____

4 Tennis would not be more popular in Germany, *(selbst wenn deutsche Spieler erfolgreicher wären.)*

____

____

5 The footballer couldn't have continued to play, *(wenn sein Bein wirklich gebrochen gewesen wäre.)*

____

6 If the word 'jogging' hadn't been invented, *(wäre das Laufen so beliebt geworden?)*

____

max. 6

gesamt max. 23

Weniger als 18 Punkte? Wenn ja, arbeite bitte Kapitel 4 nochmals durch!

5 Das Passiv

A Formen

B Verben mit zwei Objekten

C Verben des Sagens und Denkens

A Formen

		Subjekt	Form von *be*	Partizip Perfekt	
❶	*Simple present:*	The Internet	**is**	**used**	by many people.
❷	*Present progressive:*	New websites	**are being**	**designed**	all the time.
❸	*Present perfect:*	The Internet	**has been**	**made**	safer.
❹	*Simple past:*	The first computer	**was**	**built**	in the 1940s.
❺	*Past progressive:*	Disks	**were still being**	**produced**	when the CD-ROM was invented.
❻	*Past perfect:*	Experts	**had been**	**asked**	to solve the problem.
❼	*Will-future:*	Electronic media	**will be**	**used**	in the future.
❽	*Hilfsverben:*	Pocket calculators	**can be**	**made**	very cheaply.

- ▶ Das Passiv wird aus der entsprechenden Form von *be* und dem Partizip Perfekt gebildet.
- ▶ Wie im Deutschen verwendet man das Passiv, wenn nicht betont werden soll, **wer** etwas tut. In Passivsätzen ist vor allem wichtig, **was** getan wird.

▷ Die typischen Satzbaumuster bei Aktiv und Passiv sind:

	Subjekt	Verb	Objekt	
Aktiv:	Charles Lindbergh	flew	**his plane**	from New York to Paris.
Passiv:	**His plane**	was designed		in St. Louis, Missouri.
Aktiv:	The 'Spirit of St. Louis'	carried	**Lindbergh**	safely to Paris.
Passiv:	**Lindbergh**	was given	many prizes	after his flight.

Exercise 1

Vervollständige die folgenden Sätze mit den entsprechenden Passivformen.

was used – ~~was made~~ – were invented – are used – be shaped –
has been revolutionized – were created

1 In 1869 the first plastic was made from plant cellulose *(Zellstoff)*.

2 In the 20th century new types of plastic ______________________ from chemicals found in coal.

3 Nylon ______________ to make stockings.

4 Polyesters ____________________ in the 1940s.

5 Plastics that ______________ nowadays include nail polish *(Nagellack)* and plastic bags.

6 Life at home and at work ______________________________ by plastic.

Exercise 2

Verwende in den folgenden Sätzen entweder aktive oder passive Formen im *simple past*.

1 The assembly line was invented (invent) by Henry Ford, whose factories ______________ (produce) 15 million 'Model T' cars.

2 The car that Carl Benz ______________ (design) in 1885 __________ (have) a petrol engine. His car ________________________ (not show) to the public, however, until a year later.

3 The telephone ________________________ (not design) by Edison but by Bell, although Edison ______________ (invent) such famous things as the first light bulb. In fact, several important inventions ______________________ (develop) by Edison.

4 In 1901 the first radio message ____________________ (transmit) across the Atlantic, from Newfoundland to Cornwall.

5 The Channel ____________________ (cross) by air for the first time in 1785 … in a hot air balloon!

Exercise 3

Das letzte Jahrhundert hat viele große technologische Errungenschaften erlebt. Die nächsten 50 Jahre werden wohl noch mehr bringen. Setze jeweils die richtige Form des *simple past*, *present perfect* oder *will-future* im Passiv ein.

1 In 1957 the world's first satellite, Russia's 'Sputnik 1', was launched (launch). Since then all sorts of TV and millitary satellites ____________________ (construct).

2 Perhaps a manned spaceship ____________________ (send) to Mars in the next few years.

3 Astronauts ____________________ (send) to all the planets, but spacecraft probably ____________________ (not fly) as far as the stars themselves.

4 In 1927 the Atlantic ____________________ (cross) by Lindbergh alone in his plane the 'Spirit of St. Louis'.

5 A cure *(Heilmittel)* for AIDS ____________________ (not find) yet, but many illnesses ____________________ (make curable = *heilbar*) in the last 100 years. It's certain that a cure for AIDS ____________________ (discover) one day.

6 PCs ____________________ (develop) in the last century. Since then they ____________________ (improve) steadily.

7 The first atomic bomb ____________________ (drop) on Hiroshima in August 1945. Thousands of people who ____________________ (not kill) immediately in the explosion died instead from the fallout weeks later. Let's hope that in the future radioactivity ____________________ (not use) against people any more.

8 Computer systems ____________________ (change) completely by the microchip since it ____________________ (put) on the market in 1969.

B Verben mit zwei Objekten

	Subjekt	Verb	indirektes Objekt	direktes Objekt
Aktiv:	They	gave	**her**	a PC.
Passiv:	**She**	was given		a PC.

▶ Im Englischen kann das indirekte Objekt zum Subjekt eines Passivsatzes werden. Im Deutschen bevorzugt man einen Aktivsatz mit „man“:
Man gab ihr einen PC.

▷ Verben, die häufig zwei Objekte haben, sind:
ask, give, offer, promise, send, show, tell.

Exercise 4

Bei einer Pressekonferenz stellen einige Reporter einem Minister Fragen zu verschiedenen technischen Projekten. Vervollständige die Antworten des Ministers durch eine entsprechende Passivform im *simple present, simple past* oder *will-future*.
Das unterstrichene Wort wird jeweils zum Subjekt des Passivsatzes.

Minister, is it true that …

1 *Reporter* … the Prime Minister told you to stop the development of the new rocket system?
Minister No, I wasn't told to stop the development of the new rocket system.

2 *Reporter* … you've shown him plans for a new Concorde?
Minister No, ______________________ plans for a new Concorde.

3 *Reporter* … you'll ask the French to invest more in the new European spaceship?
Minister Yes, ______________________ to invest more in the new European spaceship.

4 *Reporter* … you gave other European states money to help build a space shuttle?
Minister Yes, ______________________ money to help build it.

5 *Reporter* … the Prime Minister has offered you the new job of Space Minister?
Minister No, ______________________ the new job.

6 *Reporter* … you give us a lot of wrong answers at press conferences?
Minister Oh no, ______________________ wrong answers – only correct ones!

C Verben des Sagens und Denkens

❶ **It's said/expected** that a new space shuttle will cost billions.
(Man sagt/erwartet, dass …)

❷ Einstein's ideas **are said to be** hard to understand.
(Einsteins Ideen sollen angeblich …)

- ▶ Bei Verben wie *believe, suppose, consider, expect, know, report, say, think* kann man eine Passivkonstruktion mit *it is … that* bilden ❶. Solche Formen kommen vor allem in Berichten vor, wenn der Verfasser neutral und unbeteiligt bleiben will.
- ▶ Recht häufig aber verwendet man als Alternative eine Passivkonstruktion wie in ❷, bei der ein Infinitiv mit *to* angeschlossen wird.

Exercise 5

Ein Mitarbeiter im Pentagon in Washington gibt einem Journalisten einer großen Wochenzeitschrift anonyme Insiderinformationen über militärische Geheimprojekte.

Was steht später in der Zeitschrift?
Vervollständige die folgenden Sätze mit der entsprechenden Passivform.

1 The Star Wars project *is said to* have failed.

2 New lasers for medical technology ______________________ be under development.

3 A new type of fighter aircraft ______________________ .

4 The President ______________________ against a new type of fighter aircraft.

5 The Pentagon ______________________ a new radar system.

6 The British ______________________ against a new international development project.

Test

Übersetze die fehlenden Satzteile

✔ = richtig ✘ = falsch

1 Terrorism is being fought *(wird bekämpft)* on an international level. ✔

2 A new type of laser ______ *(wird gerade entwickelt).*

3 The computer system ______ *(muss repariert werden).*

4 In future, aircraft ______ *(werden … gebaut werden)* by robots.

5 ______ *(Ihm wurde … gezeigt)* a new PC yesterday.

6 In 1877 ______ *(wurde der erste Kanaltunnel begonnen).*

7 Flight times ______ *(sind nicht reduziert worden).*

8 ______ *(mir ist … angeboten worden)* a new job.

9 Disk drives for PCs ______ *(werden nicht mehr hergestellt werden).*

10 Music ______ *(kann … gespielt werden)* on a computer.

11 The theory of genetic engineering *(Gentechnik)* ______ *(wird ihm gerade erklärt).*

12 The new medicine ______ *(soll angeblich … sein)* dangerous.

13 The hovercraft ______ *(man erwartet nicht, dass … ankommt)* on time.

14 The new spaceship ______ *(wird gerade getestet).*

15 Countries ______ *(man glaubt nicht, dass … haben)* the know-how to deal with international food shortages.

16 Tomorrow ______ *(werden mir … gezeigt)* the plans for the project.

17 The Americans ______ *(es ist bekannt, dass sich … interessieren)* in exploring *(erforschen)* Mars.

Weniger als 14 Punkte? Wenn ja, arbeite bitte Kapitel 5 nochmals durch! max. 17

6 Das Gerundium

A Gerundium als Subjekt und Objekt

B Gerundium nach Verben und Wendungen

C Gerundium nach Präpositionen

A Gerundium als Subjekt und Objekt

❶ **Living** in New York is expensive.
❷ **Owning** a Cadillac is a real status symbol.
❸ I don't mind **waiting**.

▶ Die *-ing*-Form spielt verschiedene Rollen, je nach Funktion. Hier ist sie ein Gerundium.
Das Gerundium ist eine grammatische Form, die es im Deutschen nicht gibt. Sie entspricht in etwa einem substantivierten Infinitiv (*living* = das Leben), kann aber auch durch einen Nebensatz übersetzt werden *(In New York zu leben)*. Das Gerundium kann Subjekt ❶ ❷ oder Objekt ❸ eines Satzes sein.

Exercise 1

Die folgenden Sätze stammen aus einem Reiseführer über New York. Vervollständige sie durch ein Gerundium. Suche jeweils das passende Verb aus.

drive – plan – ~~travel~~ – visit – stay – look down

1 *Travelling* on the subway is cheap and easy.
2 ______________ from the top of the Empire State Building gives you a great view of New York.
3 ______________ around at night is best by taxi.
4 ______________ in a hotel in Manhattan can cost a fortune!
5 ______________ a tour of the city is simple with this guide!
6 ______________ the Statue of Liberty is a must!

B Gerundium nach Verben und Wendungen

❶ I can't **imagine leaving** a wonderful place like San Francisco.
❷ It's **no use complaining** the whole time!

▶ Das Gerundium steht als Objekt nach bestimmten Verben ❶:

avoid	(ver)meiden	*give up*	aufgeben	*mind*	etwas dagegen haben
carry on	weitermachen	*go on*	weitermachen	*miss*	vermissen
consider	erwägen	*imagine*	sich vorstellen	*practise*	üben
deny	abstreiten	*keep (on)*	weitermachen	*quit*	aufhören
enjoy	gern tun, genießen	*look forward to*	sich freuen auf	*risk*	riskieren
finish	aufhören (mit)			*suggest*	vorschlagen

▶ Das Gerundium steht auch nach bestimmten Ausdrücken ❷:

it's (no/good) fun	es macht (keinen/viel) Spaß	*it's (not) worth*	es lohnt sich nicht
it's no good	es ist zwecklos	*How/What about …?*	Wie wärs, wenn …?
it's no use	es ist zwecklos		

Exercise 2

John und Ruth Dunderwood sind ein Seniorenpaar, das dem Stress des Großstadtlebens entkommen wollte. Deswegen sind sie vor kurzem nach Shendac, einer ruhigen Kleinstadt in der Nähe von Yosemite, umgezogen. In einem Interview mit der Ortszeitung „Yosemite Star" nannten sie einige Gründe für ihre Entscheidung, umzuziehen.

Vervollständige die folgenden Sätze mit einem Gerundium.

1 *John* I never enjoyed living (live) in Brooklyn. I'm the sort of guy that has always preferred ____________ (be) in the fresh air and ____________ (camp) in the forest, you know.

2 *Ruth* And I didn't want to go on ____________ (breathe) in that New York smog all my life, especially after I'd given up ____________ (smoke).

3 *John* You know, I just couldn't quit ____________ (think) about the forests. But it's no use ____________ (look) for that in New York! So, I suggested ____________ (move) to Shendac. We both felt it was

worth ____________________ (make) a new start here. We didn't mind ____________________ (leave) the smog and noise behind us!

4 *Ruth* John is right. It's fun ____________________ (spend) your free time in a clean environment. We're both glad we risked ____________________ (come) here.

Exercise 3

Übersetze diese Sätze und verwende dabei das Gerundium.

1 Herr Stone hörte auf zu rauchen und Alkohol zu trinken.

____

2 Ruth and Betty übten Gitarre spielen.

____

3 Fußball spielen ist Toms liebstes Hobby.

____

4 Die Feuerwehrleute riskierten, ihr Leben zu verlieren.

____

5 Mick reitet gern.

____

6 Eleanor hörte auf zu schreien.

____

C Gerundium nach Präpositionen

❶ **By learning** English you'll increase your career opportunities *(Berufsaussichten)*.
❷ Jill is **excited about spending** her vacation in Arizona.
❸ Kirk has always **dreamed of visiting** a Navajo reservation and nothing will **prevent** him **from going** this fall.
❹ A lot of Indians have no **chance of getting** a better job.

▶ Nach Präpositionen steht das Verb immer im Gerundium ❶.
Ausnahme: Die Präposition *to* deutet in der Regel darauf hin, dass ein Infinitiv folgt, aber nicht bei *look forward to*.

▷ **Präpositionen + Gerundium:**

after	nach, nachdem
before	bevor, vor
besides	abgesehen davon, dass
by	durch, wenn, indem
in spite of	obwohl
instead of	(an)statt
on	bei, als
without	ohne

! ▶ Das Verb steht auch im Gerundium nach Präpositionen, die verbunden sind mit einem Adjektiv ❷, Verb ❸ oder Substantiv ❹.

▷ **Adjektiv mit Präposition + Gerundium:**

be afraid of	Angst haben vor	*be proud of*	stolz sein auf
be good/bad at	gut/schlecht sein in	*be tired of*	etw. leid sein
be crazy about	verrückt sein nach	*be used to*	etw. gewohnt sein
be fed up with/of	genug haben von	*be sick of*	etw. satt haben
be pleased about	sich freuen über	*be worried about*	sich sorgen über

▷ **Verb mit Präposition *(prepositional verbs)* + Gerundium:**

apologize for	sich entschuldigen für	*feel like*	Lust haben auf/zu
believe in	glauben an	*insist on*	bestehen auf
blame sb for	jdn. beschuldigen	*prevent sb (from)*	jdn. abhalten von
consist of	bestehen aus	*succeed in*	Erfolg haben bei/mit, es schaffen
decide against	sich entscheiden gegen	*stop sb (from)*	jdn. abhalten von
depend on	abhängen von	*talk about/of*	sprechen über/von
dream about/of	träumen über/von	*thank sb for*	jdm. danken für

▷ **Nomen mit Präposition + Gerundium:**

chance of	Gelegenheit zu	*possibility of*	Möglichkeit zu
danger of	Gefahr zu	*reason for*	Grund zu
difficulty (in)	Schwierigkeiten zu	*risk of*	Risiko zu
hope of	Hoffnung auf	*trouble (in)*	Problem(e) mit

Exercise 4

In Kalifornien wohnen viele Einwanderer aus Mexiko.
Was halten sie von ihrem Leben in den Vereinigten Staaten?
Hier sind Meinungen, die in einer Sendung in Radio 1 San Diego ausgestrahlt wurden.
Vervollständige die folgenden Sätze mit Präposition und Gerundium.

'You're listening now to Radio 1 San Diego with facts and opinions about what life is like for Mexican immigrants in the USA.'

1 I'm proud _of being_ (be) Mexican and I refuse to apologize __________ (look) and __________ (feel) Mexican.

2 I'm sick __________ (worry) about money and how to feed my kids.

3 Well, there's no danger __________ (stay) poor. So far I've had no trouble __________ (find) work.

4 We're looking forward __________ (return) to Tijuana.
Nothing can stop us __________ (leave) San Diego.

5 In the States everybody has a real chance __________ (succeed). I want to thank lots of people __________ (help) me.

6 I don't feel __________ (say) much on the radio. I'm afraid __________ (get) into trouble with the cops *(Polizei, US)*.

Test

Exercise 1

Vervollständige die folgenden Sätze mit Präposition und Gerundium.

✔ = richtig ✘ = falsch

1 We've decided against going (go) to Chinatown. ✔

2 I'm worried ______________ (flunk, US = *durchfallen*) my exams.

3 There's no danger ______________ (lose) your way.

4 We're really looking forward ______________ (watch) the baseball game.

5 Americans believe ______________ (work) very hard – just like Germans!

6 I'm tired ______________ (look) for a parking space, and there's no possibility ______________ (get) one on Fifth Avenue.

7 Stop Jim ______________ (eat) all the peanuts before I get to the party!

max. 7

Exercise 2

Formuliere die Sätze neu, indem du eine Präposition mit Gerundium einsetzt.

1 After the accident everybody blamed the bus driver because he broke the speed limit.
After the accident everybody blamed the bus driver for breaking the speed limit. ✔

2 Melissa is proud that she is an American citizen.
Melissa is proud ______________ an American citizen.

3 Katy apologized because she was late. Katy apologized ______________ late.

4 Susan is really fed up. She shares an apartment with a very messy girl.
Susan is really fed up ______________ an apartment with a very messy girl.

5 My mum always complains that my dad is untidy.
My mum always complains ______________ my dad ______________ untidy.

6 My parents are so pleased that they won the lottery.
My parents are so pleased ______________ the lottery.

7 I'm sorry that I shouted at you yesterday. I'm sorry ______________ at you yesterday.

Weniger als 10 Punkte? Wenn ja, arbeite bitte Kapitel 6 nochmals durch!

max. 6

gesamt max. 13

7 Das Partizip

A Partizip Präsens und Partizip Perfekt

B Das Partizip Präsens anstelle von Relativsätzen

C Das Partizip Präsens oder der Infinitiv nach *see, watch, listen to, . . .*

D Partizip Präsens nach *come, sit, . . .*

A Partizip Präsens und Partizip Perfekt

❶ Her **soothing voice** got her the job as receptionist.
❷ Michael looked better when he didn't have **dyed** hair.
❸ We were late for the concert because we were stuck in **slow-moving** traffic.
❹ The **newly-wed** couple stayed in the honeymoon suite.
❺ Jill bought a **machine-made** jumper.

- ▶ Das Partizip Präsens *(present participle)* und das Partizip Perfekt (*past participle* = 3. Form) können wie ein Adjektiv vor einem Nomen stehen ❶ ❷. Auch Fügungen, in denen das Partizip Präsens oder das Partizip Perfekt mit einem Adjektiv ❸, einem Adverb ❹ oder einem Nomen ❺ eng verbunden sind, stehen vor dem dazugehörigen Nomen.
- ▶ Das Partizip Präsens hat aktiven, das Partizip Perfekt passiven Charakter.

Exercise 1

Setze das *present participle* oder das *past participle* der Verben in Klammern ein.

1 The school needs a Spanish-____________________ (speak) teacher.

2 Look at your ____________ (tear) jumper! Your mum will be angry with you!

3 Can you hear the sound of ____________________ (break) glass?

4 We looked at the ____________________ (fall) leaves on the sidewalk.

5 Dave picked up the ____________________ (break) bottle.

B Das Partizip anstelle von Relativsätzen

❶ The girl **wearing** a hat is my friend Kelly.
(The girl that/who is wearing …)

❷ Zoe got an invitation from the boy **standing** over there.
(… the boy that/who is standing …)

❸ Photos **taken** at the meeting were published
(Photos that were taken …)

- Durch die Partizipien *wearing, standing* und *taken* haben wir den Relativsatz verkürzt. Das Partizip steht normalerweise hinter (nicht vor) dem Nomen, auf das es sich bezieht.
- Das Partizip Präsens hat auch hier aktive Bedeutung: Es drückt aus, dass jemand etwas macht ❶ ❷.
  Das Partizip Perfekt hat auch hier passive Bedeutung: Es drückt aus, das mit dem Beschriebenen etwas gemacht wurde ❸.

Exercise 2

Verkürze diese Sätze durch ein Partizip Präsens.

1 Joan is watching a boy who is skateboarding in the half pipe.
Joan is watching a boy skateboarding in the half pipe.

2 Anyone who is planning to watch this movie must be crazy.
Anyone ______________________ to watch this movie must be crazy.

3 The couple that is standing over there seem to be having an argument.
The couple ______________________ over there seem to be having an argument.

4 The path which leads to the park is blocked by a fallen tree.
The path ______________________ to the park is blocked by a fallen tree.

5 The boy who is swimming over there is my cousin.
The boy ______________________ over there is my cousin.

6 The people who are sitting at the next table must be tourists.
The people ______________________ at the next table must be tourists.

Exercise 3

Übersetze die unterstrichenen Satzteile ins Englische und verwende dabei das Partizip Präsens oder das Partizip Perfekt.

1 Die Geschenke, die auf dem Tisch liegen, gehören Kevin.

The presents lying on the table belong to Kevin.

2 Das Auto, das auf der anderen Straßenseite geparkt wurde, blockiert unsere Garage.

The car ______________________________ is blocking our garage.

3 Die Leute, die letztes Jahr eingestellt *(employ)* wurden, wurden jetzt entlassen.

The people ______________________________ have now been sacked.

4 Der Mann, der in der Wohnung oben wohnt, hat drei Katzen.

The man ______________________________ has three cats.

5 Die neuen Häuser, die in unserer Straße gebaut werden, sehen schön aus.

The new houses ______________________________ look nice.

C Das Partizip Präsens oder der Infinitiv nach *see, watch, listen to, ...*

❶ She **listened to** the band **playing** the whole afternoon.
❷ We **saw** the pop star **walking** to his favourite café. *(... wie der Popstar ...)*
❸ We **saw** the pop star **walk** to his favourite café. *(... dass der Popstar ...)*
❹ They **watched** him **move** into the spotlight, **say** hello to the fans and **sing** his latest song.

- Nach Verben der Sinneswahrnehmung wie *see, watch, listen to, look at, hear, feel, smell* usw. steht im Englischen oft Objekt (z. B. in Satz 1 *the band*) + Partizip Präsens.
- Will man den **Ablauf einer Handlung** betonen, verwendet man in der Regel das **Partizip Präsens** ❶ ❷.
- Will man ausdrücken, dass eine **Handlung beendet** wurde, verwendet man in der Regel den **Infinitiv ohne *to*** ❸.
- Folgen **mehrere Handlungen aufeinander**, verwendet man auch den **Infinitiv ohne *to*** ❹.

Exercise 4

Setze entweder das Partizip Präsens oder den Infinitiv ein. (Manchmal musst du überlegen, welche Lösung am besten in den jeweiligen Zusammenhang passt.)

~~get~~ – ~~speak~~ – drive – play – complain – hit – burn – open – take – sit – switch

1 I saw one member of the band _get_ into a huge car, _speak_ to his girlfriend and then ________________ away.

2 Betty listened to him ______________________ his guitar for hours and hours.

3 When we arrived at the party we heard some of the neighbours ______________________ about all the noise.

4 I suddenly felt something ___________ me on the head, and I fell to the ground.

5 Paul stopped his motorbike because he thought he smelt something ________________ .

6 The police watched the young man ________________ the door of the bar, ____________ out a cigarette and ______________ down next to the woman.

7 I noticed a girl ________________ on her walkman immediately after the lesson.

Exercise 5

Verbinde die Sätze – je nach Bedeutung – durch ein Partizip Präsens oder den Infinitiv ohne *to*.

1 Amy watched Bob and Tom. They were playing football.
Amy watched Bob and Tom _playing_ football.

2 Sarah heard her brother. He was shouting for help.
Sarah heard her brother ________________ for help.

3 I saw Liz. She crossed the road and disappeared into her house.
I saw Liz ________________ the road and ________________ into her house.

4 As I walked past the school I heard the band. They were practising a song.
As I walked past the school I heard the band ________________ a song.

5 James could smell the pizza. It was baking in the oven.
James could smell the pizza ________________ in the oven.

6 David saw a police car. It stopped outside his house.
David saw a police car ________________ outside his house.

D Das Partizip Präsens nach *come, sit, …*

❶ **He came racing** along the road.
(… kam … entlanggerannt)
❷ John **sat listening** to his new CD.
(… saß und hörte … an)

▶ Nach Verben der Bewegung (*come, go, walk* usw.) und Verben der Ruhe (*sit, stand, lie* usw.) verwendet man im Englischen das **Partizip Präsens**.

Exercise 6

Übersetze.

1 Die Hooligans kamen ins Stadion gelaufen.

The hooligans came running into the stadium.

2 Robert lag am Strand und schlief.

____

3 Zitternd vor Aufregung *(with excitement)* standen die Mädchen den ganzen Tag vor dem Aufnahmestudio *(recording studio)*.

____

____

____

4 Der Hund kam aus dem Wagen gesprungen.

____

5 Am Abend saß Jenny zu Hause und spielte auf ihrem Computer.

____

____

6 Die Kinder liefen weinend nach Hause.

____

Test

Exercise 1

Setze entweder das Partizip Präsens oder den Infinitiv ein.
(Überlege dir, welche Lösung am besten in den jeweiligen Kontext passt.)

✔ = richtig ✘ = falsch

shake – run – throw – disappear – knock – play

1 Did you notice his hands ______________________________ the whole time during the exam?

2 The police saw the fans _____________ onto the football field, ________________ some bottles at the players and then ________________________________ into the crowd.

3 Pat felt the boat suddenly ___________________ against something.

4 We could hear somebody _____________________ the same CD again and again.

max. 6

Exercise 2

Die folgenden Sätze beschreiben Ereignisse bei einem Erdbeben.
Verbinde die Sätze. Setze entweder den Infinitiv oder das Partizip Präsens ein.

1 People were screaming. I heard them.

I heard ______________________________ .

2 A house collapsed. I saw it.

I saw a house ______________________________ .

3 The earth shook. I felt it.

I felt ______________________________ .

4 People were shouting for help. I heard them.

I heard ______________________________ for help.

5 Something was burning. I could smell it.

I could smell something ______________________________ .

6 Fire engines raced round the corner, drove down the street and disappeared again. I saw them.

I saw fire engines ____________________ round the corner, ____________________ down the street and ______________________________ again.

7 People were digging in the ruins. I saw them.

I saw people ______________________________ in the ruins.

8 A little boy was looking for his parents. I noticed him.

I noticed a little boy ______________________________ .

9 An ambulance arrived. I saw it.

I saw an ambulance ______________________________ .

10 The soldiers were giving people food. I watched them.

I watched the soldiers ______________________________ people food.

11 A man stole food from a lorry. I saw him.

I saw a man ______________________________ food from a lorry.

max. 13

Weniger als 15 Punkte? Wenn ja, arbeite bitte Kapitel 7 C und D nochmals durch!

gesamt max. 19

8 Relativsätze

A Bestimmende Relativsätze

❶ 'Bio-X' is the muesli **that/which** keeps you healthy!
❷ The girl **that/who** won the marathon is only 15.
❸ Rick has got lots of friends **whose** parents go jogging.
❹ The distance **(that/which)** I usually run is five miles.

- Ein bestimmender Relativsatz bezieht sich auf ein Wort und bestimmt dieses Wort genauer.
  Ohne einen bestimmenden Relativsatz würden die Beispielsätze keinen Sinn machen und es wäre nicht klar, wer oder was gemeint ist: welche Müslisorte ❶, welches Mädchen ❷, welche Freunde ❸, welche Laufstrecke ❹?
  Ein bestimmender Relativsatz darf niemals durch Komma, Gedankenstrich usw. vom restlichen Satz abgetrennt werden.

- Bei Personen und bei Tieren, zu denen wir eine persönliche Beziehung haben, stehen die Relativpronomen *that, who, whose* (dessen, deren) ❷ ❸.
  Bei Dingen und bei Tieren allgemein stehen *that, which, whose* ❶ ❹.

- In Sätzen, in denen das Subjekt des Hauptsatzes nicht gleichzeitig das Subjekt des Relativsatzes ist, muss kein Relativpronomen stehen ❹. Solche Relativsätze heißen *contact clauses*.

Exercise 1

Lies den Text sorgfältig durch. Verbinde dann die darauf folgenden Satzteile miteinander anhand der Informationen im Text.

KEEP FIT – DON'T SMOKE!

Smoking is a dangerous habit, and cancer *(Krebs)* can be the result. Only a minority of young people smoke these days – for most teenagers it's not a popular or acceptable habit.

But why do some young people start smoking? It often happens in families where children see their parents smoking, or in cases where a boyfriend or girlfriend smokes. The cigarette firms prefer to use adverts with only young, healthy people in them, although the firms in fact sell a very unhealthy product. And unfortunately a lot of young people are persuaded *(überreden)* by the 'cool' image in the adverts – probably a friend of **yours** is among them.

So remember: If you want to keep fit and healthy – **don't** smoke!

Welche Satzteile gehören zusammen?

1	Smoking is a habit	**a**	whose parents smoke
2	It's only a minority of young people	**b**	the cigarette firms prefer to use
3	For most teenagers smoking isn't something	**c**	who smoke these days.
		d	the cigarette firms sell
4	Those young people … often start themselves because they see their mother or father doing it.	**e**	the cigarette firms have persuaded to smoke with their 'cool' advertising image.
5	A girl … will probably start smoking just like him.	**f**	which can cause cancer.
		g	that is popular or acceptable.
6	The adverts … show only healthy young people.	**h**	whose boyfriend smokes
		i	that wants to keep fit
7	The product … is very unhealthy.		
8	A lot of us have got a friend		
9	Anybody … shouldn't smoke!		

1 f **2** ____ **3** ____ **4** ____ **5** ____ **6** ____ **7** ____ **8** ____ **9** ____

Exercise 2

Kannst du die drei *contact clauses* in Übung 1 finden?
Schreibe die Satznummern auf.

Satz ________, ________, ________.

Exercise 3

Setze *who, which, that, whose* ein.
Verwende ein Relativpronomen nur da, wo es tatsächlich notwendig ist.
(Und vergiss nicht: Manchmal gibt es mehr als eine Einsetzmöglichkeit.)

1 It's a drink that/which helps your skin to look good.

2 It's something ______________ tastes great!

3 It's the drink ______________ you need to feel great.

4 It's drunk by runners ______________ want to win races.

5 It's perfect for a person ______________ job is full of stress.

6 It's wonderful for mothers ______________ are tired after a day with the kids.

7 It's ideal for the career *(Karriere)* woman ______________ life is always busy.

8 It's got all the vitamins ______________ we need for the winter, so there's nothing ______________ is more important in cold weather.

9 So why not recommend ENERGYDRINK to all the people ______________ you know?

B Nicht bestimmende Relativsätze

1. Jill, **who** is trying to lose weight, usually goes to the sauna after work.
2. Weight-lifting, **which** lots of women do now, is very popular these days.
3. Mr Jones drinks far too much, **which** isn't good for his heart.

▶ Nicht bestimmende Relativsätze enthalten zusätzliche Informationen. Im Gegensatz zu bestimmenden Relativsätzen könnte man sie weglassen, ohne dass die Aussage des Satzes sinnlos wird.
Bei dieser Art von Relativsätzen sind Kommas notwendig.

- Bei Personen und bei Tieren, zu denen wir eine persönliche Beziehung haben, stehen die Relativpronomen *who, whose* ❶; bei Dingen und bei Tieren allgemein stehen *which, whose* ❷.
- Das Relativpronomen kann sich auf den ganzen vorausgehenden Satz beziehen und wird dann mit „was“ übersetzt ❸.

Exercise 4

In der Fernsehsendung „Looking Good“ diskutieren vier Expertinnen über Diät und Gewichtsverlust. Hier sind einige ihrer Bemerkungen.

Setze jeweils das richtige Relativpronomen ein und vergiss nicht, die Kommas zu setzen.

1 *Jean* I think that weight, which can be a terrible problem, gives some women real complexes. One of my best friends, whose name I can't mention here, has got so many complexes because of it.

2 *Mary* You need a lot of discipline to lose weight ________________ isn't easy.

3 *Sue* My daughter ____________________ has been on a diet for four months now is looking so much better.

4 *Sarah* Dr Roger Hammer _________________________ book 'The Hammer Diet' I can really recommend suggests 800 calories a day for 12 weeks.

5 *Sue* People often eat more than they really need ________________ is what often makes normal people fat and fat people fatter!

6 *Jean* Fifteen minutes in the sauna ______________________ is something lots of women enjoy is certainly a great way to stay slim *(schlank)*.

7 *Mary* I find that older people ____________________ should really know better eat far too much fast food. And fast food ___________________ is simply full of calories is so bad for your skin!

C Relativsätze mit Präpositionen

❶ This is the cream **(that/which)** I clean my skin **with**.
❷ This is the cream **with which** I clean my skin.
❸ Mrs Hammer, **who** Dr Roger Hammer developed his famous diet **for**, lost a lot of weight.

▶ In der Regel steht die Präposition an derselben Stelle wie in einem Hauptsatz ❶ ❸. Vergleiche:

(Hauptsatz)
I clean my skin with this cream.

(Relativsatz)
This is the cream that/which **I clean my skin with**.

Im formellen Englisch kann die Präposition auch vor dem Relativpronomen stehen ❷.

Exercise 5

Vervollständige die folgenden Sätze, indem du in jeden Relativsatz die richtige Präposition und das richtige Relativpronomen einsetzt.

1 *which, who, whose; on, for, in*

It was the hardest race _which_ I've ever taken part _in_.

2 *who, whose, which; to, on, with*

John, __________________ I run the health-food shop *(Naturkostladen)* __________________, is my best friend.

3 *who, which, whose; at, in, on*

You're the one person __________________ help I'm really dependent __________________.

4 *which, who; about, on, after*

This is the only point __________________ she insists __________________.

5 *who, that, whose; at, with, about*

Here's the wholemeal bread *(Vollkornbrot)* __________________ I told you __________________.

6 *which, that, who; for, after, without*

Her boss, __________________ she'd worked __________________ all her life, retired last month.

Test

Der große amerikanische Skiläufer Norman Willy erzählt aus seinem Leben in einem Interview für Radio Stern in München.
Er verrät dem Interviewer sein Rezept für Allround-Fitness.

Setze *who, which, that, whose* nur da ein, wo ein Relativpronomen erforderlich ist. Manchmal ist mehr als eine Lösung möglich.

✔ = richtig ✘ = falsch

There's nothing ________________ [1] I enjoy as much as cross-country skiing *(Langlauf)*, ________________ [2] is a great way to stay fit.

The distance ________________ [3] is best for me is about 20 miles, ________________ [4] can be hard if you try to do it every day. Anybody ________________ [5] loves being physically active will know that gymnastics is something ________________ [6] gives you a great feeling. For people ________________ [7] lives are spent in an office, some sort of exercise (________________ [8] it's always possible to find a bit of time for) is really necessary. My sister's old boyfriend, ________________ [9] name I can't remember now, often used to go swimming with me years ago, ________________ [10] was great fun and much better than exercising alone. The energy ________________ [11] he had was amazing – and the speed ________________ [12] he swam at was amazing, too. It made a big impression. He was the first man ________________ [13] I ever met ________________ [14] was a truly great swimmer.

I'm somebody ________________ [15] fitness is very important for. And my girlfriend, ________________ [16] it's just as important for, was the one ________________ [17] persuaded me to start professional skiing. I also do a lot of weightlifting, ________________ [18] is something ________________ [19] I like a lot.

Weniger als 15 Punkte? Wenn ja, arbeite bitte Kapitel 8 nochmals durch!

max. 19

9 Modale Hilfsverben

A Notwendigkeit/Verbot

B Aufforderung/Ratschlag

C Fähigkeit/Möglichkeit

D Gewohnheit

A Notwendigkeit/Verbot

❶ People **must/have to** eat to stay alive
❷ I **must** do some exercise. (I want to)
❸ I **have to** do some exercise. (doctor's orders)
❹ You are **not allowed to** drive faster than 70 mph in England.
❺ You **mustn't** play in the street. *(darfst nicht)*
❻ You **don't have to/don't need to/needn't** drive so fast – we're not late! *(brauchst nicht)*

- *Must* wird nur für die Gegenwart verwendet. Für alle anderen Zeiten verwendet man eine Form von *have to*.

- Um eine **Notwendigkeit** (= müssen) auszudrücken, ist *have to* im amerikanischen Englisch die gebräuchlichere Form.
  Im britischen English können *must* oder *have to* verwendet werden ❶.

- Um eine **Verpflichtung** (= müssen) auszudrücken, ist *have to* im amerikanischen Englisch die gebräuchlichere Form. Im britischen English wird *must* oft verwendet, um die Gefühle und Wünsche des Sprechers und Hörers auszudrücken, beispielsweise, um Anweisungen zu geben oder zu erbitten ❷. *Have (got) to* wird im britischen Englisch meistens verwendet, um über Notwendigkeiten zu sprechen, die von „außen" herangetragen werden, beispielsweise durch Gesetze, Bestimmungen oder die Befehle anderer Leute ❸.

- Um ein **Verbot** auszudrücken (= nicht dürfen), wird *not allowed to* oder *mustn't* verwendet, bei Geboten *must*. Dabei ist *not allowed to* die sachlichere Form ❹ und *must/mustn't* eine Mischung aus persönlichem Befehl und Ratschlag ❺.

- *Don't have to, don't need to* und *needn't* im Sinne von „nicht brauchen" sind gleichbedeutend ❻.

Exercise 1

Valerie Shaw („Val“) ist 17 Jahre alt, kommt aus Edinburgh und war neulich für drei Monate bei ihrem amerikanischen Vater Tim zu Besuch in New York.
Tim hat ihr ein paar nützliche Tipps über die Stadt gegeben.

Setze *must/have to* oder *mustn't* ein.

'There are some things you really _must/have to_ see in this city, Val.

You ____________ [1] go on a tour of Chinatown, for example, and you ______________ [2] take a boat trip around the Statue of Liberty ... But be careful – you ______________ [3] use the subway late at night, and you _______________ [4] carry a lot of money in your purse *(Handtasche, US)* – it's too dangerous.

Exercise 2

Val brauchte von ihrem Vater ein paar praktische Informationen über das Telefonieren in den USA.

Setze die richtige Form von *(not) have to* im *simple present* ein.

Val How much _do_ I _have to_ pay here for a local call, Dad?

Tim It costs 25c and all you _______________ [1] do is this – you _________________ [2] lift the receiver and put in the money. Then you __________________ [3] dial the number. Usually you ____________ _________________ [4] go via *(über)* the operator *(Telefonist/in)* and you _____________________ [5] put in money to get directory assistance, either – that's always free here!

Exercise 3

Was hat Val bei ihrem Telefonat in den USA machen müssen?
Setze die richtige Form von *(not) have to* im *simple past* ein.

First she <u>had to</u> read the instructions in the phone booth *(Telefonzelle, US)* carefully. Afterwards she __________ [1] lift the receiver, and then she __________ [2] insert *(einwerfen)* the correct money. Once that was done, Val __________ [3] dial the number she wanted. She also __________ [4] call directory assistance to get some information, but as that's free in the USA she __________ [5] pay a cent for it!

Exercise 4

Bevor Val nach New York geflogen ist, hatte sie von Tim einen Brief mit einigen nützlichen Vorschlägen bekommen.

Setze eine entsprechende Form von *(not) have to* im *will-future* ein.

You'<u>ll have to</u> bring your trainers *(Turnschuhe)* if you want to join the fitness freaks in Central Park, Val. You __________ [1] go out and buy lots of cotton clothes – it's hot here in summer! Most tourists don't need a visa, so you __________ [2] apply for one. You __________ [3] worry about getting around – public transport in New York is great. And you __________ [4] learn American English, either, although some New Yorkers are hard to understand!

Exercise 5

Der Lebensstil in den USA ist etwas anders als in Europa.

Übersetze die fehlenden Satzteile mit *mustn't, not allowed to* oder *needn't/not need to.*

1 American teenagers <u>needn't/don't need to</u> do *(brauchen nicht)* military service.

2 You __________ drive *(man darf nicht)* faster than 65 mph in the USA.

3 You __________ use *(man braucht nicht)* you car in Washington because public transport is so good, but you __________ walk *(man darf nicht)* the streets of LA – it's too dangerous.

4 Tourists __________ take *(dürfen nicht)* fresh produce into the USA.

5 You __________ smoke *(nicht dürfen)* in most American restaurants.

B Aufforderung/Ratschlag

❶ Sue **should/ought to** accept that job. *(sollte)*
❷ You **shouldn't** smoke so much. *(solltest nicht)*
❸ You'**d better** be on time, or we'll miss the beginning of the concert.
(Es wäre besser, wenn du …)
❹ You'**d better not** be late again, or you'll be fired!
(Es wäre besser, wenn du nicht …)

- Mit *should* und *ought to* werden **Aufforderungen** und **Ratschläge** formuliert ❶. In verneinten Sätzen steht immer *shouldn't* ❷.
- *Had better (not)* wird vorwiegend in gesprochenem Englisch verwendet, wenn unangenehme Folgen zu befürchten sind, falls man einem Rat nicht folgt. Mit *had better (not)* kann der Ratschlag fast einer Warnung nahe kommen ❸ ❹.

Exercise 6

Was sollte man in New York möglichst vermeiden, damit man nicht Opfer von Gewalt wird? Ein Freund gibt Valerie Ratschläge.

Übersetze die fehlenden Satzteile mit einer entsprechenden Form von *should(n't), ought to, had better (not)*. Manchmal sind zwei Lösungen möglich.

It's a great city! But you'll enjoy your vacation more if you remember a few simple rules.

1 You _shouldn't use_ the subway alone after 10 p.m.
(Man sollte … nicht benutzen)

2 You' _d better_ ________________ a lot of money on you.
(Es wäre besser, nicht … zu tragen)

3 You ________________________ to strangers.
(Es wäre besser, … nicht zu reden)

4 ________________________ a taxi at night.
(Es wäre besser, … zu nehmen)

5 ________________________ a friend exactly when you intend to come home at night.
(Man sollte … sagen)

6 ________________________ when you go into the Bronx.
(Du solltest … vorsichtig sein)

7 ____ into cheap bars.

(Man sollte nicht … hineingehen)

8 ____ your car unlocked.

(Man sollte nie … lassen)

C Fähigkeit/Möglichkeit

❶ You **can** find more Germans in New York than you **can** in Frankfurt!
❷ In the last century millions of immigrants **were able to** start a new life in the USA.
❸ **Could** you understand what he said on the phone yesterday?
– No, I **couldn't**.
❹ We **might/may/could** move to Detroit next year. *(werden vielleicht, könnten)*

!

- *Can* und *be able to* drücken eine **Fähigkeit** oder **Unfähigkeit** aus. Die Ersatzform von *can (be able to)* wird in der Gegenwart viel weniger verwendet als *can* ❶.
- *Could* bezeichnet eine **Fähigkeit**, die in der Vergangenheit vorhanden war. Soll ausgedrückt werden, was jemand in der Vergangenheit einmal tun konnte und tatsächlich auch getan hat, muss man *was/were able to* (im Sinne von „fähig", „in der Lage sein") verwenden ❷. Sonst ist es mit *could* weitgehend austauschbar.

  Could ist bei **Fragen** und **Verneinungen** immer richtig ❸.
- *May* und *might* drücken aus, dass eine **Möglichkeit** besteht oder bestehen könnte, die man eventuell nutzen wird. *May* und *might* sind dabei weitgehend austauschbar ❹.

Exercise 7

Übersetze die fehlenden Satzteile mit einer entsprechenden Form von *can* oder *could* und dem Infinitiv.

1 You can find *(kann … finden)* more Italians in New York than in Venice, but you ____________ *(kann nicht … bekommen)* such good pizzas in New York!

2 ____________ *(wir konnten … nicht besuchen)* Carnegie Hall last year. – Oh, why ____________ you? *(konnten … nicht)*

3 How ____________ *(können wir erreichen)* the UN from here?

4 ____________ *(er konnte uns nicht sagen)* how big Washington is.

Exercise 8

Eine beliebte Fernsehsendung heißt „Did You Know …?". Der Showmaster Bob Bishop eröffnet gerade eine neue Sendung.

Setze eine entsprechende Form von *(not) be able to* im *simple past, present perfect* oder *will-future* ein.

1 In 1624 the Dutch were able to buy Manhattan Island from the Indians for only $24!

2 Of course, the Indians ____________ ____________ buy it back so far!

3 If you go up the Empire State building in the lift, you ____________ reach the top in no time!

4 In 1973 Coleman A. Young ____________ ____________ become the first black mayor of Detroit, but no black man ____________ become President yet.

5 The USA probably ____________ ____________ produce any more oil after about the year 2040.

Exercise 9

Weißt du noch?

Vervollständige die folgenden Fragen mit der entsprechenden Form von *(not) be able to.* Versuche, die richtige Lösung zu den Fragen zu unterstreichen, ohne die Übung Nr. 8 anzuschauen!

1 How much _were_ the Dutch _able to_ buy Manhattan Island for?

$42 / $360 / $2400 / $24

2 Who ________________ become Detroit's first black mayor in 1973?

Coleman A. Young/Stevie Wonder/George Bush

3 Who ____________________ win full civil rights for black Americans?

Loretta King/Michael Jackson/Martin Luther King

4 After which year ________________ the USA ________________ produce any more oil?

2001 / 2114 / 2040 / 2140

Exercise 10

Peter ist nicht ganz sicher, wie er die letzten Tage seines Aufenthalts an der amerikanischen Westküste verbringen soll.

Schreibe vollständige Sätze mit *may, might, could.*

1 take a trip to LA/might/Peter

Peter might take a trip to LA.

2 may/Or/spend a few days in Seattle/he

____

____

3 be able to stay there/He thinks he/more than three days/might not

____

____

4 to have three days in LA instead?/be more fun/Could/it

____

____

D Gewohnheit

❶ Indians **used to live** on Manhattan Island. *(lebten früher)*
❷ **Didn't** he **use to teach** at our high school? *(Hat er nicht früher … unterrichtet?)*
❸ After a few weeks Valerie **was used to** the American accent.

▶ *Used to/didn't use to* gibt es nicht im Präsens und Futur, sondern nur in der Vergangenheitsform. *Used to/didn't use to* ist für alle Personen gleich.

Used to drückt eine gewohnheitsmäßige Handlung in der (oft ferneren) Vergangenheit aus, die sich kaum wiederholen wird ❶ ❷.

▶ *To be used to something* bedeutet „an etwas gewöhnt sein" ❸.

Exercise 11

Wie hat Val ihre drei Monate in New York verbracht?

Setze *used to* oder *didn't use to* ein.

'Well, I *used to* spend a couple of mornings every week at a super little café in Greenwich Village.… Sometimes dad and I ______________ [1] meet for lunch in Chinatown, or we ______________ [2] go to Little Italy and eat a pizza there.… I ______________ [3] jog quite a lot in Central Park, but I ______________ [4] go out much at night at first. In fact, I ______________ [5] like the city at all at night – but once I was used to it I didn't find it so scary.

Test

Exercise 1

Übersetze die fehlenden Satzteile mit *must, mustn't* oder *don't need to/needn't* und dem Infinitiv.

✔ = richtig ✘ = falsch

1 You ______________________ *(darfst nicht … verwenden)* Canadian coins for the phone – only US coins.

2 You ______________________ *(brauchst nicht … zu reden)* to the operator to make a local call.

3 You ______________________ *(darfst nicht … zu Fuß gehen)* through Central Park late at night.

4 You ______________________ *(brauchst nicht … zu besorgen = get)* a visa to enter this country.

5 You ______________________ *(brauchst nicht … zu fahren)* your car in San Francisco – the subway system, called BART (Bay Area Rapid Transport), is great.

max. 5

Exercise 2

Setze eine entsprechende Form von *(not) have to* ein.

1 Tomorrow morning I ______________ fly to Denver – I'm meeting someone there.

2 Nobody in our tour group ______________ change *(umtauschen)* more than € 250 so far.

3 Why ______________ millions of Irish people ______________ leave their country in the 19th century?

4 When we go to the States next year we ______________ take a tent – we're going to go camping. But we ______________ hire a car there – Uncle Bob will lend us his old Pontiac.

max. 5

Exercise 3

City Hall *(Rathaus, US)* befindet sich am südlichen Ende von Manhattan. Von dort aus wird die ganze Stadt verwaltet. Eine Bürgerinitiative hat einige Vorschläge und Wünsche aus der Bevölkerung an die City Hall gerichtet.

Übersetze die fehlenden Satzteile mit *should(n't)* oder *ought to* und einem Infinitiv. Die beiden Formen sind austauschbar.

1 City Hall ______________________________ *(sollte nicht … bauen)* the new airport on Staten Island.

2 City Hall ______________________________ *(sollte … abreißen* = tear down*)* the slums in the Bronx.

3 City Hall ______________________________ *(sollte … beschäftigen)* more doctors in our hospitals.

4 City Hall ______________________________ *(sollte nicht … ausgeben)* so little on our schools.

5 City Hall ______________________________ *(sollte … tun)* more to stop corruption.

max 5

Exercise 4

Setze die richtige Form von *(not) be* able to ein. Wo ein (*) steht, setze die verneinte Form ein.

1 What was the name of the general who ______________________________ win independence for the American colonies in the 18th century?

2 ________________ a black person ________________ become President in the 21th century?

3 Jimmy (*) ______________________________ repair his car so far.

4 I (*) ______________________ go to the movies last night.

max. 4

Weniger als 15 Punkte? Wenn ja, arbeite bitte Kapitel 9 nochmals durch!

gesamt max. 19

10 Der Artikel

A	Nomen mit und ohne Artikel
B	Geografische Bezeichnungen und Zeitangaben
C	Feste Wendungen mit/ohne *the*
D	Unterschiede im Gebrauch von *a/an*
E	Feste Wendungen mit/ohne *a/an*

A Nomen mit und ohne Artikel

❶ **Violence** is a problem in most big cities.
❷ **The violence** in parts of London is increasing.
❸ **Breakfast** is the only meal at which I eat **bread**.
❹ **The breakfast** I had in that hotel in Miami was the biggest I've ever eaten.
❺ **Oil** is an important mineral.
❻ **The oil** they found in our region is exported.
❼ **Children** like **animals**.
❽ **The children** next door take their dog for a walk every day.

- Abstrakte Nomen stehen **ohne** bestimmten Artikel, wenn sie in einem allgemeinen Sinn gebraucht werden ❶.
- Auch Bezeichnungen für Mahlzeiten und Stoffnamen wie beispielsweise *bread, oil* stehen **ohne** bestimmten Artikel ❸ ❺.
- Ebenso stehen Gattungsnamen im Plural **ohne** bestimmten Artikel ❼.
- Alle oben genannten Nomen stehen aber **mit** Artikel, wenn jemand oder etwas speziell gemeint ist und durch *of*-Fügungen oder Relativsätze näher bestimmt ist ❷ ❹ ❻ ❽.

Exercise 1

Setze den Artikel ein, wo er notwendig ist.

1 The pollution of Germany's rivers was killing all the fish.

2 More and more people are beginning to realize the importance of ________ sport.

3 ________ hunger and ________ poverty *(Armut)* in some regions of the world are hard to imagine.

4 ________ chemistry one learns at school is not enough to understand ________ pollution of the atmosphere properly.

5 I hate ________ noise and ________ smoke, so I rarely go to cafés.

6 If you want ________ peace, you must not prepare for ________ war.

7 ________ death of Martin Luther King was a tragedy for the world.

8 Buddhists see both ________ birth and ________ death as parts of ________ life.

9 David usually eats toast and marmalade for ________ breakfast.

10 Sometimes ________ people work too hard.

Exercise 2

Übersetze die fehlenden Satzteile.

1 After lunch *(nach dem Mittagessen)* the President gave a press conference.

2 ______________________ *(die Industrie)* is polluting ______________________ *(die Umwelt)*.

3 ______________________ *(der Alkoholismus)* is worse in Sweden than in England.

4 I like ______________________ *(die Popmusik)*, but ______________________ *(der Lärm)* that Rod Cool produces hurts my ears.

5 ______________________ *(das Brot)* used to be cheap in Germany.

6 Ireland struggled for years for ______________________ *(die Unabhängigkeit)*.

7 ______________________ *(die Religion)* always has a lot of influence on ______________________ *(die Gesellschaft)*.

8 Many parents protest against ______________________ *(die Gewalt)* which is shown on TV every evening.

9 ______________________ *(das Benzin)* becomes more expensive every year.

10 Drugs are a danger to ______________________ *(die Gesellschaft)*.

B Geografische Bezeichnungen und Zeitangaben

❶ **On Saturday** I'm going to go to **Oxford Street**.
❷ My birthday is in **January**.
❸ After **school** I went to **the hospital** to see my girlfriend.
She's been in **hospital** for three weeks now.
❹ **Mount Everest** is in **the Himalayas**.
❺ **The USA** has more nuclear arms than **Russia**.

- Im Gegensatz zum Deutschen stehen die Wochentage und Monate immer **ohne Artikel** ❶ ❷, ebenso die meisten Straßennamen und Bergnamen ❶ ❹.
- Bei *church, hospital, prison, school* und *university* usw. steht **kein Artikel**, wenn es um **den Zweck des Gebäudes** geht, d. h. um Gottesdienst, Krankenhausaufenthalt, Gefängnisstrafe, Unterricht in der Schule und Studium. Wenn es um **das Gebäude selbst** geht, steht der **Artikel** ❸.
- Alle geografischen Namen **im Plural** stehen mit Artikel: *the Himalayas, the United States of America* ❹ ❺.
- Bei geografischen Bezeichnungen (Flüsse, Berge, Länder) **im Singular** und bei Zeitangaben gibt es keine festen Regeln für den Gebrauch des Artikels.

▷ Folgende Bezeichnungen stehen

ohne Artikel:	**mit** Artikel:
England, France, Italy, Poland, Switzerland	the United States, the Netherlands
Regent's Park, Tower Bridge	the High Street, the Golden Gate Bridge
Buckingham Palace, Heathrow Airport	the British Museum, the White House
Mount Everest, Loch Ness	the Rocky Mountains, the Alps

Exercise 3

Richtig oder falsch?
Streiche die falsch gesetzten Artikel in den unterstrichenen Wendungen durch.

1 Terrorists are often isolated when they are in ~~the~~ prison.

2 I never go to the church on the Sunday, but my grandparents usually do.

3 The Mont Blanc is the highest mountain in the Alps.

4 The USA was once thought to be a land of unlimited opportunities.
People emigrated in past centuries from the England, the Switzerland and the Netherlands to start a new life there.

5 After the accident the injured man was taken to the hospital, where he had a two-hour operation.

6 The Oxford Street is famous for its shops.

7 It is strange to think of people in the Australia lying in the sun at the Christmas, because in that part of the world the December is in the summer.

8 I'm working hard for my A-levels, and every day I walk past the university on my way to the school and wish I was a student instead of a schoolgirl.

C Feste Wendungen mit/ohne *the*

❶ **All the clothes** I bought in London last year were of very poor quality.
All clothes are very expensive these days.

❷ I'm surprised that **most people** like computer games. **Most of the games** I know are boring.

❸ I usually go to school **by bike**, but sometimes I go **by bus** or **by car**.

❹ **Half (of) the** people in our group paid **double the** amount of money for a hotel room **twice the** size of ours.

❺ John has been **on the phone** for half an hour now.
Marc's learning to **play the guitar**. He's already given a concert **on the radio** and he'll be **on TV** next week.

❻ The boss gave his secretary **permission** to have the morning off **in case** she needed to arrange for a babysitter.

❼ Don't disturb him when he's **at work**. And don't ring him up when he's **in bed**.

- Der bestimmte Artikel **steht** hinter *all*, wenn „alle" aus einer bestimmten Anzahl gemeint sind. Der Artikel **steht nicht**, wenn *all* eine allgemeine Bedeutung hat ❶.
- Hinter *most* **steht kein** bestimmter Artikel, wenn es „die Mehrheit/ der größere Teil" bedeutet. Hinter *most of* **steht** der Artikel. Vor *most of* **steht kein** Artikel ❷.
- Der bestimmte Artikel **steht** nicht bei der Bezeichnung eines Verkehrsmittels ❸.
- Der bestimmte Artikel **steht** hinter *half (of), double* und *twice* ❹.
- Für viele Wendungen gibt es leider keine Regeln über den Gebrauch des Artikels. Man muss die Wendungen auswendig lernen ❺ ❻ ❼.

Exercise 4

Ein Reporter telefoniert mit der Redaktion und gibt die Zeitungsüberschriften für die morgige Ausgabe der Zeitung durch.

Vervollständige diese Schlagzeilen, indem du die angegebenen Wendungen übersetzt.

1 **MURDERER** ___in prison___ **AT LAST!**
(im Gefängnis)

2 **Children Protest:**
We Don't Learn Anything ____________
(in der Schule)

3 **Prime Minister Gave** ____________
To Shoot Terrorists! *(der Erlaubnis)*

4 GHOST APPEARS ____________
(im Fernsehen)

5 Pop star tells his life story:
I never learnt to play ____________
(die Gitarre)

6 **Scientific Research:**
____________ **Sleep Too Much!**
(die meisten Leute)

7 HACKERS ____________ IN CENTRAL BANK COMPUTER!
(bei der Arbeit)

8 US President will visit GB ____________
(im Februar)

9 **BANK ROBBERY:** ____________ **FOUND!**
(das meiste Geld)

10 **Scandal! Minister spends**
____________ **on new missile system!**
(die doppelte Summe)

D Unterschiede im Gebrauch von *a/an*

❶ Sarah's father is **a politician** in Belfast. – Is he **a Catholic**?
❷ The skier raced down the slope *(Piste)* at 90 **kilometres an hour**.
❸ I bought a model of Buckingham Palace **as a souvenir**.
❹ **What a** surprise! John's girlfriend is **quite a** famous singer!
❺ You'll have to start wearing **glasses** soon.
❻ I've got **some** useful **advice** for you.

- Im Gegensatz zum Deutschen stehen im Englischen Bezeichnungen der Zugehörigkeit zu Beruf, Konfession, Partei **mit** dem unbestimmten Artikel ❶.
- Mengenangaben mit der Bedeutung „pro" stehen im Englischen **mit** dem unbestimmten Artikel. Im Deutschen verwendet man statt „pro" auch den bestimmten Artikel (z. B. *90 kilometres an hour* = 90 Kilometer pro/die Stunde, *1.5 euros a pound* = 1,5 Euro das (pro) Pfund) ❷.
- Nach *as* steht im Englischen der unbestimmte Artikel (z. B. *as a souvenir* = als Souvenir) ❸.
- Nach *quite, such, rather* und nach *what* in Ausrufen vor zählbaren Begriffen steht im Englischen der unbestimmte Artikel. Beachte die Wortstellung ❹!
- Bei den Nomen, die im Englischen als Plural behandelt werden (z. B. *glasses, scissors, trousers*), steht kein unbestimmter Artikel ❺.
- Bei unzählbaren Substantiven (z. B. *advice, information, news*) steht im Englischen kein unbestimmter Artikel ❻. Meistens verwendet man sie mit *some* oder *any*.

Exercise 5

Setze den unbestimmten Artikel da ein, wo er erforderlich ist.

1 My sister is ________ schoolteacher. She often complains that she needs ________ glasses to read her pupils' handwriting!

2 Last Christmas my boyfriend gave me one of his favourite sweaters as ________ present.

3 I am always glad to get ________ news from my Australian relations.

4 Can I wear ________ jeans to your party, or would it be better to wear ________ smart *(chic)* trousers?

5 It was such ________ disappointment to hear what ________ terrible weather was forecast *(vorhersagen)* on TV for the weekend.

6 The first time I was in an English pub I ordered half ________ pint of ________ beer. I didn't realize that one pint was only half ________ litre!

7 If you were ________ Catholic in Northern Ireland, would you support the IRA?

8 They chose ________ really good music for that TV advert.

E Feste Wendungen mit/ohne *a/an*

❶ I'm **in a hurry** today, so will you **give me a ring** tomorrow?
❷ Can you **give me a hand** with my luggage? It's very heavy.
❸ Is there a chemist's nearby? I've got **a temperature** and **a terrible headache**. I hope I haven't got **flu**.
❹ After practising for four hours **without a break**, the guitarist decided to listen to some cassettes **for a change**.
❺ **As a rule**, politicans can't discuss political matters **in a friendly way** with each other.
❻ Our English teacher speaks **in a loud voice** and expects us to **take an interest**.
❼ The Victorian era **came to an end** with the death of Queen Victoria.
❽ Our industry is responsible for pollution **to a high degree**. Few private people are **in a position** to reduce it.

▶ Für diese Wendungen – und leider für viele mehr – gibt es keine Regeln über den Gebrauch des unbestimmten Artikels. Die Wendungen müssen einfach auswendig gelernt werden.

Exercise 6

Max Brumm, ein deutscher Autofahrer, ist in einen Verkehrsunfall auf der Autobahn M40 in der Nähe von Oxford verwickelt.
Nach dem Unfall versucht er den Hergang des Unfalls zu beschreiben. Alison, eine Studentin aus Oxford, dolmetscht für ihn.

Vervollständige ihre Übersetzung, indem du die unterstrichenen Satzteile ergänzt. Benutze jeweils eine Wendung mit dem unbestimmten Artikel.

1 *Max* Ich war furchtbar in Eile, weil ich um 8 Uhr einen Termin in Oxford hatte. Ich fuhr schon sehr lange ohne Unterbrechung.

Alison The driver was ________________________ because he had an appointment in Oxford at 8 o'clock. He had been driving for ________ ________________________________.

2 *Max* In der Regel fahre ich nicht über 70 Meilen/Std., aber infolge eines technischen Fehlers *(defect)* war ich nicht in der Lage, meine Geschwindigkeit zu messen.

Alison ____________________ he doesn't drive faster than ____________________ ______________, but ____________________________ a technical defect he was _________________________________ to measure his speed.

3 *Max* Ich hatte Kopfschmerzen und im Radio erzählte eine Frau mit lauter Stimme von einem langweiligen Aufenthalt in Wales. Ich glaube, ich bin dann eingeschlafen. Was für ein schrecklicher Unfall! Ein Glück, dass niemand verletzt wurde.

Alison He had _______________________ and on the radio a woman was talking __________________________ about a boring holiday in Wales. He thinks he fell asleep. ________________ terrible accident! He says it's lucky that nobody was injured.

Test

Exercise 1

Setze den bestimmten Artikel *(the)* ein, wo er notwendig ist.

✔ = richtig ✘ = falsch

1 ________ time is ________ money.

2 We use ________ oil for heating and ________ gas for cooking.

3 ________ electricity we need for our hot water all comes from solar cells.

4 ________ Canary Islands are off ________ coast of Africa.

5 Would you like to come to ________ dinner on ________ Saturday? I'm going to cook ________ fish and ________ chips.

6 The thief spent ten years in ________ prison.

7 ________ most people watch ________ TV almost every evening.

8 James is interested in ________ art.
He studied ________ architecture at ________ university,
and later specialized in design.
Now he works at ________ art college in ________ Oxford Street.

max. 19

Exercise 2

Setze den unbestimmten Artikel *(a/an)* ein, wo er notwendig ist.

1 Have you got ________ headache? My sister is ________ nurse; perhaps she can help.

2 Keep this ring as ________ souvenir of the days we've spent together.
What ________ wonderful time we've had!

3 Ben doesn't wear ________ glasses, although his eyesight is bad.

4 Mr Coon came to school in ________ pyjamas yesterday! He thought he was wearing ________ trousers, and he got such ________ shock when he took his coat off! We didn't stop laughing for at least half ________ hour.

max. 9

Exercise 3

Setze *the, a, some* oder *any* ein, wo sie erforderlich sind.

1 __________ milk costs about 60 cents __________ litre in __________ Germany. What does it cost in __________ USA?

2 Let me give you __________ advice: go to __________ Turkey for your holiday. __________ weather there is sure to be good, and __________ people you meet are all so kind and helpful.

3 __________ sale of __________ alcohol should be banned in football stadiums, where __________ violence is such __________ problem.

4 __________ economy will improve if __________ oil is found.

5 __________ Ben Nevis is the highest mountain in __________ Highlands of ______ Scotland. What is the highest mountain in __________ USA?

6 My mother went to __________ school on parents' day and asked my teachers for __________ information about a suitable career for me. She hopes that I'll go to __________ university, but I would rather learn to play __________ guitar and become __________ rock musician.

7 On __________ Sunday I went to visit a friend who's been in __________ hospital since her accident in __________ January.

max. 26

Weniger als 43 Punkte? Wenn ja, arbeite bitte Kapitel 10 nochmals durch!

gesamt max. 54

11 Adverbien und Adjektive

A Adverbien

❶ He spoke **angrily** about the silly TV adverts.
❷ It's **simply** amazing how much is spent on commercials.
❸ They filmed the car ad **fantastically** well.
❹ **Unfortunately**, nobody liked the slogan.
❺ If you work **extra** *(Adverb)* at weekends, you should get **extra** *(Adjektiv)* money for it.

▶ Das Adverb beschreibt Verben ❶ ❺, Adjektive ❷, andere Adverbien ❸ oder auch einen ganzen Satz ❹.

▷ Bei der Bildung eines Adverbs aus einem Adjektiv verwandeln sich:

angr**y**	angr**ily**	simp**le**	simp**ly**	bas**ic**	bas**ically**
bus**y**	bus**ily**	probab**le**	probab**ly**	econom**ic**	econom**ically**
dr**y**	dr**ily**	sensib**le**	sensib**ly**	fantast**ic**	fantast**ically**

Aber:

sh**y**	sh**yly**	whol**e**	whol**ly**	publ**ic**	publ**icly**

▶ Adjektive, die auf *-ly* enden *(friendly, lonely, lovely, silly …)*, bilden keine Adverbien mit *-ly*. Stattdessen benutzt man eine Adverbialbestimmung mit *way/manner* z. B. *in a friendly way*.

▶ *Daily, weekly, monthly, yearly* sowie *early, extra* (zusätzlich), *fast, straight* (gerade), *low* (niedrig) können entweder als Adjektive oder als Adverbien verwendet werden.

Exercise 1

Hier ist ein Entwurf für eine Informationsbroschüre der Trinity High School.

Adverb oder Adjektiv? Achte bei den Lösungen auf die richtige Form des Adverbs.

Welcome to Trinity High School!

This school was opened in 1953 and has a (long) __long__ [1] tradition of exam success.

We accept pupils at age 11 and hope they will leave us at 18 as (academic) ____________ [2] and (professional) ____________ [3] (successful) ____________ [4] young adults. However, we do not (simple) ____________ [5] focus on (academic)____________ [6] subjects, but try and turn our pupils into (social) ____________ [7] and (environmental) ____________ [8] aware young people.

Students can benefit from a number of (interesting) ____________ [9] clubs and societies at Trinity. The school is set in (beautiful) ____________ [10] grounds with (careful) ____________ [11] laid out gardens surrounding an (old) ____________ [12] Tudor manor house. We pride ourselves on having a (friendly) ____________ [13] and (relaxed) ____________ [14] atmosphere and hope we can welcome you here next year.

Exercise 2

Unterstreiche alle Adverbien im Text oben.
Wie viele kannst du finden?

B Adverbien mit zwei Formen

❶ The commercial was **pretty** *(ziemlich)* stupid, but at least the girl in it smiled **prettily** *(hübsch)*.

❷ He works so **hard** *(schwer, hart)* that we **hardly** *(kaum)* see him any more.

▷ Einige Adverbien haben zwei verschiedene Formen, wobei jede Form eine eigene Bedeutung hat. Die wichtigsten sind:

direct	*direkt*	directly	*gleich, sofort*
free	*umsonst*	freely	*frei, freimütig*
high	*hoch (hinauf)*	highly	*höchst*
late	*spät*	lately	*in letzter Zeit*
most	*am meisten*	mostly	*meistens*
near	*nahe (heran)*	nearly	*beinahe, fast*
deep	*tief*	deeply	*zutiefst*

Exercise 3

Hier ist der Entwurf einer Zeitschriftenreklame für das exklusive Parfüm „Tropical Night“. Vervollständige den Entwurf durch ein Adverb mit oder ohne *-ly*.

TROPICAL NIGHT ... Do you want to fully experience just how highly [1] (high) attractive you are? Then try this new perfume, which more and more women have been using ____________ [2] (late). It's a perfume that will make your partner move ____________ [3] (near) to you when he comes home ____________ [4] (late) at night. A quality perfume that doesn't come ____________ [5] (free), but it's worth that little extra. Use it ____________ [6] (free) to enjoy its full tropical fragrance *(Duft)*.

TROPICAL NIGHT ... the perfume the modern woman likes ____________ [7] (most), and one that a woman ____________ [8] (most) uses to create an exotic atmosphere. Try it and you'll feel yourself flying ____________ [9] (high) into a warm, tropical night and ____________ [10] (near) everything will suddenly seem perfect.

TROPICAL NIGHT the perfume for you.

C Adjektiv anstatt Adverb

❶ The results of the survey look **interesting**.
❷ It's becoming **difficult** to sell our products abroad.
❸ That curry smells **bad** and tastes **awful**!

▶ Mit den Verben *appear, be, feel, look, smell, sound, taste* und mit allen Verben, die dem deutschen „werden" entsprechen *(become, get, go, grow)*, benutzt man ein Adjektiv statt eines Adverbs.

Exercise 4

Adjektiv oder Adverb?

Vervollständige die folgenden Werbesprüche.

1 T.O.P. jeans look ___great___ (great) and feel ______________ (perfect). Better start wearing them ______________ (regular), OK?

2 'Big Wheel' hamburgers taste just ______________ (wonderful)! So eat a 'Big Wheel' ______________ (slow) and ______________ (careful)! Mmmmmm!!!

3 Are there days at work when you get ______________ (tired) or grow ______________ (angry) much too ______________ (quick)? Don't worry – you're not going ______________ (crazy). But you do need to relax ______________ (proper), and 'Vitadrink' will help you in ways you never dreamed of. If it sounds ______________ (unbelievable), why not try it for yourself?

Test

Adjektiv oder Adverb?

Setze die richtige Form des in Klammern angegebenen Adjektivs ein.

✔ = richtig ✘ = falsch

1 – I think people in commercials don't talk ________________ (natural).
– I agree – they speak ____________________________ (silly) the whole time, don't they?

2 The jet flew ________________ (straight) and ________________ (low) over the busy airport.

3 The ________________ (new) car was presented ________________ (public) yesterday.

4 That idea sounds ________________ ________________ (unusual/exciting). I feel ________________ (certain) it'll appear ________________ (interesting) to our readers as well.

5 Of course a ________________ (monthly) magazine is printed ________________ (monthly)!

6 He's such a ________________ (boring) teacher – he talks ______________ (dry) and never makes a single joke.

7 I ______________ (near) feel sick whenever she comes ______________ (near) me with that perfume of hers!

8 The Southampton train goes ________________ (direct), so you won't have to change anywhere.

9 He spoke ________________ (angry) and hurt her ________________ (deep).

10 People can't walk around ________________ (free) in a safari park.

Weniger als 16 Punkte? Wenn ja, arbeite Kapitel 11 nochmals durch! max. 20

Her mit den besseren Noten!

Das bewährte **Besser in ...-Lernhilfenprogramm** gibt es komplett in Neuausgabe für Deutsch, Englisch und Mathematik von Klasse 5 – 10: Je ein vierfarbiger Band pro Fach und Jahrgang deckt alle wichtigen Lehrplanthemen ab.

Übungen, Tipps, Lösungshilfen und die wichtigsten Regeln zum Nachschlagen und Lernen für zu Hause und unterwegs. Mit separatem Lösungsheft – zur Selbstkontrolle oder für die Eltern.

	ISBN 3-589-
Deutsch 5. Klasse	21809-6
Deutsch 6. Klasse	21811-8
Deutsch 7. Klasse	21812-6
Deutsch 8. Klasse	21813-4
Deutsch 9. Klasse	21814-2
Deutsch 10. Klasse	21815-0

	ISBN 3-589-
Englisch 5. Klasse	21816-9
Englisch 6. Klasse	21817-7
Englisch 7. Klasse	21818-5
Englisch 8. Klasse	21819-3
Englisch 9. Klasse	21820-7
Englisch 10. Klasse	21821-5

	ISBN 3-589-
Mathe 5. Klasse	21822-3
Mathe 6. Klasse	21823-1
Mathe 7. Klasse	21825-8
Mathe 8. Klasse	21826-6
Mathe 9. Klasse	21827-4
Mathe 10. Klasse	21828-2

Die folgenden Titel liegen weiterhin in zweifarbiger Ausstattung vor:

	ISBN 3-589-
Französisch Grammatik 1. Lernjahr	21831-2
Französisch Grammatik 2. Lernjahr	21832-0
Französisch Grammatik 3./4. Lernjahr	21833-9
Latein Grammatik 1./2. Lernjahr	21830-4
Spanisch Grammatik 1./2. Lernjahr	21829-0

Cornelsen
Power Learning

Fragen Sie bitte in Ihrer Buchhandlung!